'Vladimir Mayakovsky' and Other Poems

VLADIMIR MAYAKOVSKY was born in 1893 in Baghdati, a village in Georgia. Following the death of his father in 1906, the family moved to Moscow. Mayakovsky was an active Communist from an early age, and in 1909 served an eleven-month jail sentence for revolutionary activities. During his imprisonment, aged sixteen, Mayakovsky began to write. The leading Russian Futurist writer, best known for his poetry, Mayakovsky also had an immense influence on the visual arts, cinema, drama and general culture of the early Soviet period. He committed suicide in 1930.

JAMES WOMACK was born in Cambridge in 1979 and studied English, Russian, and translation at university. He currently lives in Madrid, where he helps to run Nevsky Prospects, a publishing house specialising in Spanish translations of Russian literature. He has translated widely from Russian and Spanish into English and Spanish, both independently and in collaboration with his wife, the writer Marian Womack. Among his published translations are works by Silvina Ocampo, Roberto Arlt, Sergio del Molino, Ivan Turgenev, and Gaito Gazdanov. His translation of Mayakovsky's essays on cinema was published in 2013 as *Escritos sobre cine*. He contributed translations of Vladimir Mayakovsky and Velimir Khlebnikov to the *Penguin Book of Russian Poetry* (2015). A collection of his own poems, *Misprint*, was published by Carcanet in 2012.

FyfieldBooks aim to make available some of the great classics of British and European literature in clear, affordable formats, and to restore often neglected writers to their place in literary tradition.

FyfieldBooks take their name from the Fyfield elm in Matthew Arnold's 'Scholar Gypsy' and 'Thyrsis'. The tree stood not far from the village where the series was originally devised in 1971.

Roam on! The light we sought is shining still.
Dost thou ask proof? Our tree yet crowns the hill,
Our Scholar travels yet the loved hill-side

from 'Thyrsis'

VLADIMIR MAYAKOVSKY

'Vladimir Mayakovsky'
and Other Poems

Translated & edited by
James Womack

Fyfield*Books*

CARCANET

First published in Great Britain in 2016 by

CARCANET PRESS LTD
Alliance House, 30 Cross Street
Manchester M2 7AQ
www.carcanet.co.uk

We welcome your comments on our publications
Write to us at info@carcanet.co.uk

A CIP catalogue record for this book is available
from the British Library, ISBN 9781784102920

The publisher acknowledges financial assistance
from Arts Council England

Typeset by XL Publishing Services, Exmouth

Contents

Introduction

WHERE TO START with Vladimir Mayakovsky? He is a difficult figure to bring into focus. Sometimes he seems monolithic and unapproachable, unimpeachable, a monument to everything that the Soviet Union wanted to believe about itself; at other times he's merely a heap of broken images, a tall man with a loud voice, shouting about… what, exactly? Or he's a willing victim of the Soviet system, the man who said that he 'put his foot on the throat of his own song' and who suffered so much from this self-abnegation that it drove him to suicide. Or he's a martyr whose afterlife ruined him, turning him from 'merely' a popular poet into the man who, as Stalin put it, 'was, and remains, the best, most gifted poet of our Soviet epoch'. This official commendation transformed Mayakovsky into a burdensome idol: Pasternak saw Stalin's support as Mayakovsky's 'second death', after which he was forced on the public 'like potatoes in the time of Catherine the Great'. Add to this the widespread rejection of all things Soviet after the Union collapsed at the beginning of the 1990s. Where to start with Mayakovsky? Do we even *need* to start with Mayakovsky? There is now a miasma of confusion, of contradictory signals, surrounding both the man and his work.

There is no single answer to the question of how to think about Mayakovsky: biography, like translation, is above all else a matter of interpretation. All I want to suggest are two entry points. The first is Bengt Jangfeldt's *Mayakovsky: A Biography*.[1] This is a scholarly, thorough, and extremely well presented introduction, not only to Mayakovsky, but also to the intellectual currents of his time, to the circles in which he moved and, no less importantly, to the *ménage à trois* of Mayakovsky, Lilya Brik, and Lilya's husband Osip, which provided the motor for a great deal of Mayakovsky's best work. Jangfeldt admirably sets out to describe Mayakovsky as a man, rather than as a demon or figurehead. This is one way in.

The second way to approach Mayakovsky might be to look at him in action. One of the ways in which he used his vast energy was in his work for the nascent Soviet film industry. Mayakovsky wrote scripts and acted in films throughout the 1910s and 20s, though very little of his work survives. I include in this volume what I consider his best screenplay, *How's It Going?*, a work that indicates the extent to which his poetic thought spread outside the bounds of 'pure' poetry. The only complete film that remains is the silent *The Lady and the Hooligan* (1918).[2] Mayakovsky, the eponymous hooligan, starts the film as the antagonist of the eponymous lady (Aleksandra Rebikhova), and then changes his stance once he realises that Rebikhova's desire to educate the working class is a positive thing. He fights with the other mature students, who arrange to meet him after class and punish him. It is an unfair fight. Mayakovsky is stabbed. On his deathbed, he pushes aside the priest who comes to read him his last rites and calls instead for the lady, who kisses him, then watches as he dies – at length, and always aware of where he needs to roll his dying body in order to appear in the centre of the shot. This combination of an egoistic central role in the drama, the denial of traditional (religious) consolation, the belief in the redemptive power of love, and a commitment to the values of socialist labour, together with the desire for a hero's death, gives us a series of useful handholds by which we, as innocent outsiders, might get to grips with Mayakovsky.

Those are two ways in. But a brief factual biography may also be useful. Vladimir Vladimirovich Mayakovsky was born in 1893 in Baghdati, Georgia. He grew up speaking both Russian and Georgian. He was politically active from an early age and a participant in socialist demonstrations by age fourteen. Mayakovsky's father, a forester, died young: blood poisoning from pricking a finger on a rusty pin while filing papers in 1906 (hence Mayakovsky's almost pathological cleanliness in later life). The family – Mayakovsky, his mother, and two sisters – sold up and moved to Moscow the same year. There Mayakovsky went to school, got involved in socialist activism, was expelled for his inability to pay, and eventually sentenced to eleven months in prison for socialist activities. It was during his imprisonment that Mayakovsky began to write poetry. When he was released in 1911, aged eighteen, he entered the Moscow Arts School. There he met the future Futurist poet David Burliuk, who told him to keep on writing poetry. By now Mayakovsky had found his vocation: his first published poems appeared in 1912, and in the same year he was included in the Futurist manifesto *A Slap in the Face of Public Taste*. He developed a style of complicatedly rhymed, oblique, almost surrealist poetry, presenting himself to the world as a mythological figure, uniquely condemned to suffer and to redeem the world. Mayakovsky set himself up, with certain provisos, as the poet of the Revolution, and his work from this period includes numerous propaganda posters and a series of agitprop poems and plays. Between 1922 and 1928 Mayakovsky was the pre-eminent Soviet poet, moderating his style to meet an encroaching public philistinism. Perhaps he did not manage to become philistine enough. The last year or so of his life was marked by antagonism between him and his public, and in mid-April of 1930 Mayakovsky killed himself. It is unclear whether this was motivated by unhappiness with the Soviet system, unhappiness with his personal life, or some subtler existential despair.[3]

Mayakovsky's suicide was an ambiguous – albeit final – act, but his reputation was immediately leapt upon by the Soviet state, which decided, following Stalin, to make Mayakovsky *the* Soviet martyr-poet. This appropriation pointed in several directions, but its major effect was to smooth Mayakovsky's rough edges. For example, consider the poem 'To Russia': the 1950s edition of Mayakovsky's *Complete Works* deliberately fudged the poem's date, admitting that to date it to 1916, the editor's preferred choice, was 'hypothetical'. Bengt Jangfeldt shows that the poem has to date to 1917, which means that its criticisms are applicable to the early Soviet state as well as the tsarist society Mayakovsky's Soviet editors would have it attack. Little things like that.

I hope that I have read enough around and about Mayakovsky to be able to try to see him without all this baggage. In any case, I need to say a little bit about my choice of poems. I wanted to give an idea, in the space allotted to me, of the extent and variety of Mayakovsky's writing: I have included two longer poems, 'A Cloud in Trousers' and 'I Love'; a film scenario, *How's It Going?*; and a play, the modestly titled *Vladimir Mayakovsky*. There is agitprop, love poetry, public and private verse. The major missing element – if things that aren't there are what you are looking for – is Mayakovsky's extremely large-scale poetry: the forty-nine pages of *About This*, and the seventy-eight pages of his elegy *Vladimir Ilich Lenin*. In general, I think that by limiting myself in the main to poems of no longer than four or five pages, I have been able to give an idea of the kind of poet Mayakovsky was, the writer as I think it is helpful to see him.

And what kind of writer is that? Going all the way back to 1826, Goethe has an interesting letter to the Grand Duke Carl August about his idea of what a useful kind of poetry might be. Talking about a young poet who has written to him for advice, Goethe says that

> Until now he has remained inside the circle of modern, subjective, self-concerned and self-absorbed poetry. Insofar as he has to deal with anything concerned with inner experience, feelings, disposition and reflection, he does it all very well, and he will cope well with any theme in which these things are dealt with; however, as far as anything objective is concerned he has not yet fully developed his abilities, for he feels, like young writers of our time, a desire to flee from that reality on which everything imaginative must be built and to which every ideal must return. I set him the following task: to describe Hamburg as if he had just recently returned to it. He seized on the sentimental ideas of his mother, his friends, their love, patience and assistance. The Elbe remained some generic stream of silver, the port and the town were unimportant, he did not mention the crowds, and one might as well have been in Naumburg or Merseburg. I spoke to him openly about this and said that if he could add the panorama of a great northern merchant town to his feelings for home and family, then he might achieve something truly worthwhile.

Mayakovsky's is never a truly personal verse – as he writes in 'I Love', 'I grew up speaking / to buildings', an overly-literal view of domesticity – and Goethe's description is a useful way of thinking about how he writes. The external elements, the houses and villages, nature and the city, are always present in what Mayakovsky produces, even when he is describing his own heartache and despair. The 'Mayakovsky' of Mayakovsky's poems is not the

Mayakovsky of Mayakovsky's life, but rather a magnificent exaggeration, an enormous panorama of what an individual might look like if he managed to map his subjectivity onto the world that stood outside him. For Mayakovsky, the pathetic fallacy is not an artistic falsehood: the only way of explaining himself to the world is to make the world subject to his own emotions and strivings. And how does he achieve this? Chief among his weapons is an unmatched command of rhyme, unconnected to anything so banal as strict logical sense. In his poetry, especially his earlier, more avowedly Futurist work, you get the impression that he is allowing his purely verbal sense to structure his work. In *Mayakovsky's Rhyme* Mikhail Shtokmar identifies hundreds of distinctive ways in which Mayakovsky uses rhyme, from a 'perfect' variety to one in which the rhymed words are barely connected, as in the poem 'The Revolution', which rhymes 'serOyu' tangentially with 'gromo-vOye'.[4] Mayakovsky normally keeps the rhymes happy in one of two ways: either by allowing strong rhymes to control a broken rhythm – an English analogy would be Shelton Brooks's 'The Darktown Strutters' Ball' (1917), in which the couplet 'Better be ready 'bout half past eight / Now baby, don't be late' is allowed to be almost completely arrhythmical because of the absolute rhyme of eight / late – or else by allowing a regular rhythm to enforce on the ear the appearance of rhyme sounds that aren't actually there – as in Regina Spektor's lyrics to 'On the Radio' (2006), 'While we were on our knees / praying that disease / would leave the ones we loved / and never come again', in which the non-existent rhyme between 'loved' and 'again' is implied by the rhythm of the verse.

For a further example of Mayakovsky's verbal sense controlling his literal meaning, consider the beginning of the poem 'Stunning Facts'. In Russian it runs as follows (I'll set it out flat on the page, though Mayakovsky breaks the lines):

Небывалей не было у истории в аннале
факта: вчера, сквозь иней,
звеня в «Интернационале»,
Смольный ринулся к рабочим в Берлине.

One can't help but feel that the second line only includes the padding phrase 'сквозь иней' ('through the hoarfrost') in order to set up the slant-rhyme with 'Берлине' ('Berlin') in line four. Maya-kovsky's surreal imagination may at times be a byproduct of his desire to create foursquare rhyming units – setup and punchline, setup and punchline, over and again. While I was translating the poem 'Mad About the Movies' I got stuck and asked some friends for help with a particular phrase, 'огурцами огурятся'. Along with this answer ('pickling around like pickles') one correspondent pointed out that Mayakovsky 'was clearly desperate for a snappy rhyme to "курица" ("chicken"), which appears two lines further on'. It seems a fair but easily overlooked point: Mayakovsky is often content to allow sound to guide sense.

I hope that the following translations balance these conflicting demands. I have allowed myself to veer towards paraphrase at times in order to give priority to the production of things that in my opinion are valid poems in English (this is, I think – I believe – necessary when translating Mayakovsky). The source texts I used when making my translations are those of the 1955 thirteen-volume *Collected Works*. The dates given with each poem are those of compo-sition, usually following the dates in the *Collected Works*, but with occasional exceptions (such as corrections to deliberate mis-dating, described above). In cases when editorial interjection would harm the poem, but the context is indispensable to a fair reading, I have provided footnotes. Of course, some things I have doubtlessly missed, or do not know. If there are things the reader doesn't see explained, the Internet is a good first port of call.

As I hope is clear from this introduction (and, yes, from the poems), this is a personal selection of the things I like most about Mayakovsky. He is a writer who has been translated generously into English, especially in the last few years, in a series of books that gives us a number of different, equally interesting writers. My favourite translations of Mayakovsky, if this one doesn't live up to your expectations, or if you want more, are the following:

Vladimir Mayakovsky, *Mayakovsky*, translated by Herbert Marshall (New York: Hill & Wang, 1965)

Vladimir Mayakovsky et al., *Night Wraps the Sky*, edited by Michael Almereyda (New York: Farrar, Straus & Giroux, 2008)

Vladimir Mayakovsky, *Selected Poems*, translated by James H. McGavran III (Illinois: Northwestern University Press, 2013)

Vladimir Mayakovsky, *Volodya: Selected Works*, edited by Rosy Carrick (London: Enitharmon, 2015)

NOTES

1 *Med livet som insats: berlättelsen om Vladimir Majakovskij och hans krets* (Stockholm: Wahlström & Widstrand, 2007), English translation by Harry D. Watson published by University of Chicago Press, 2014.

2 *The Lady and the Hooligan* can be viewed on YouTube: www.youtube. com/watch?v=re_ytlvoUqE. If you don't have time to watch the whole thing – it is only three quarters of an hour – then the vital section for my argument is the last five minutes.

3 For more insight on Mayakovsky's death and his mood around the time (albeit from a partial source) see his brief biography *I Myself* (1922; revised edition 1928).

4 Mikhail Shtokmar, *Rifma Mayakovskogo* (*Mayakovsky's Rhyme*) (Moscow: Sovetsky Pisatel', 1958).

'Vladimir Mayakovsky'
and Other Poems

Night

Discarded and gathered the white and the crimson,
handfuls of ducats thrown on the green;
into the black palms of the reclining windows
burning yellow cards were given.

It wasn't odd for the boulevards and the square
to see the buildings dressed in dark blue togas.
And like yellow scars – this happened earlier –
the streetlamps fastened bracelets to pedestrians' legs.

The crowd, a hurrying tortoiseshell cat,
swam and twisted, was dragged through the doors;
everyone wanted to get their cut
from this lumpish heap of poured-out laughter.

I sensed the importunate paws of a skirt,
and shoved a smile right back at it. Fearing
blows against their tin façades, the card-sharps smirked,
above each eye a painted parrot's wing.

·1912·

Morning

The gloomy rain glanced
askance.
And past the defined
lines
of cables' iron thoughts –
a featherbed.
Whose head
was where

the rising stars
gently placed their feet.
The fading street-
lamps –
emperors
in crowns of gas –
just made it worse
to lay your eyes
on the feuding slew of streetwalkers.
The horror
in laughter
at mean little jokes
pokes
from the yellows
of poisonous roses
and grows
in a zig-
zag.
Past the outcry
and dismay
the eye
looks happily:
the slave
to his crossroads nailed
suffering-peaceful-indifferent,
the grave
of the brothels
thrown into a single ardent
vase, by the light from the east.

· 1912 ·

Port

The bed-sheet water under the boat's belly.
The hull's white tooth breaking on the swell.
There was a sound of funnels howling –
love and lust poured from the brass funnel.
Boats snuggled in the cradle of the slipway
up against the nipples of iron mothers.
And in the ears of the deafened steamships
there burnt, like earrings, their anchors.

·1912·

Street Scene

In the shops, filled with faces worn and rotten,
there ooze – from the wounded stalls – cranberries.
and a painted letter galloped
past me, over the moony herring.

My steps make the sleeper ties boom,
I throw buckshot into the streets' tambourine.
My steps shake the tired trams
pierced by a burning spear.

Holding its only eye up in its fist,
the twisted square prowled close.
It looked at the sky in its white gauze-mist
with its basilisky, eyeless face.

·1913·

Could You?

I straightway smudged life's dull self-portrait,
splashing the paint from a glass;
I saw the ocean's vicious cheekblades
in a dish of aspic.
On the scales of a tinny fish I read the invitation
of the future, and saw her lips.
And you
could you
play a nocturne
on a flute you've made from sluicepipes?

·1913·

Me

I.

The footsteps
            of lunatics
beat out their cruel
phrases on the worn-down
pavements of my soul.
Where cities are hanged
                and towers' crooked necks
congeal in nooses made of cloud –
I alone go out to sob
                that by the crossroads
policemen are crucified.

2.

A FEW WORDS ABOUT MY WIFE

By the distant beaches of seas unknown
passes the moon – my wife.
My redheaded love.
In her train there stretches
a rowdy crowd
of bright-striped constellations.

She haloes a motor garage
and kisses a newspaper kiosk
and the milky way is her winking pageboy
spangled with tacky stars.

And me? On fire, I carried those frozen
buckets – my eyes filled with your light – with my brow for a yoke.
Did your hips sing like an amber violin?
Did you hang in the silky surface of lakes?

Don't throw your light on these wicked roofs.
Buried under the sad sand, I drown on the boulevards:
but your daughter remains, my song, sitting
in coffee shops, in fishnet stockings.

3.

A FEW WORDS ABOUT MY MOTHER

I have a mother against cornflower-blue wallpaper.
But I go about like a particoloured peahen,
shaggy camomile, with measured pace, and suffer.
The evening strikes up its rusty oboes,
I go to the window,
                    believing
                              that I'll see once again

the cloud sown over the house.
But to my sick mother
run the people's rumours
from the bed to the empty corner.
Mother knows that heaped thoughts climb madly
from behind the roof
of the Shustov
cognac factory.
And when my brow, with its felt hat halo,
is soaked in blood by this fading window frame,
I say, my bass cutting the wind's howl:
'Mama,
if the vases of your suffering feel sorrow
for me, shattered by the heels of the cloud's dance –
who will caress the golden hands
broken by the sign in Avantso's art shop window?...'

4.

A FEW WORDS ABOUT MYSELF

I like to see children die.
Have you noticed the laughing tide,
its leading breakers
behind this solemn schnozz?
And I –
the street my
reading room – have often flicked
through the graveyard book.
Me and the broken-down fence:
midnight gave us the once-
over
with her damp fingers;
away the mad cathedral
hurtled,
with drops from a downpour

on its bald-pate cupola.
I saw Christ run away from his icon,
the sleet, weeping, kissed the wind-blown
hem of his garment.
I shout to the cement,
I plunge the blade
of frenzied words
into the puffy pulp of the sky:
'Sun! My father! You at least don't torture me!
It is my blood that you spilled, that flows off into the distance.
It is my soul in the remnants
of a shredded cloud
in the sky, burnt-out
over
the rusty cross on the bell tower!
Time!
You at least – god dauber, lame –
sketch my image
among the pantheon of the monsters of the age!
I am lonely,
like – a man going blind – the one remaining eye!'

·1913·

Exhausted Portrait of Spring

Leaves.
The tracks the fox
leaves.

·1913·

In Tiredness

Earth!
Let me press my ragged lips to your bald and healing head, or kiss
these unfamiliar golden marks.
In the smoky hair that hangs above the tinworks's blazing eyes,
let me embrace the swamp's empty dugs.
You! We are the same,
wounded, hunted by fauns,
flushed from cover by Death's whinnying horse.
Smoke from behind the house grabs at us with its long hands,
with its muddy, angry eyes that rot in the falling fire.
My sister!
In the future's almshouses
my mother will perhaps be found;
I threw her this horn that songs have bloodied.
Croaking, the ditch gallops across the field, a green bounty
hunter, and binds us
with the cords of filthy roads.

·1913·

Love

The shy girl clothed herself in swampy muck
as frogsong rose forebodingly,
and something red squirmed on the tracks;
the trains curled past reproachfully.

The wind's mazurka-wildness burnt
the cloud-couples through the smoky sunset,
and here am I, a melting July pavement,
where she throws her kisses like the butts of cigarettes.

Come on then, walk out on the city,
go naked in the sun, you dumb fucks!
Pour drunken wines into wineskin-titties,
pour rain-kisses onto your coal-cheeks.

·1913·

We

crawl the earth under the eyelashes of fallen palmtrees
to poke out the deserts' goggly eyes;
we crawl the canals' shrivelled lips
to catch at dreadnaughts' smiles.
Stop right there, anger!
Onto this bonfire of kindled constellations
I won't let you hurl my crazy decrepit mother.
Road – hell's drinking-horn – confuse with your wine the
snoring goods carts!
Make the volcanoes' nostrils wide with drunkenness!
We'll throw moulted angel feathers onto our beloveds' hats;
we'll cut feather boas from the comets that stumble through space.

·1913·

Cries and Whispers

Noises come through the echoing city,
the thunder of wheels and the whisper of boots,
but people and horses are nothing but jackboys,
following the courses of runaway plaits.

Here come the delicate noises that girls make.
Here come the carts with their boxes of booms.
A gelding trots by in its whispering tunic.
Huge rolls of thunder spill out of the trams.

The whole busy square swims through the arcade
along the canals where thoughts criss-cross,
where noise with its skew-whiff and soot-smeared face
is crowned the king of all the bazaars.

·1913·

Up Yours!

Out to the clean street in an hour's time will flow
you humanoid shapes in slumped and blubbery grease:
I will have opened the jewelbox of all these poems,
prodigal and spendthrift of words without price.

Look at you, gent with cabbage in your beard –
leftover soup you couldn't be bothered to eat;
look at you, lady smeared with thick white lead,
an oyster in a shell made from silver plate.

Clamber over this butterfly that is the poet's heart,
all of you, filthy people, with shoes and shoeless.
The crowd is turning animal, it's all going to start,
the legs are all bristling on the hundred-headed louse.

And if today I'm hunnish, don't feel any tug
to primp and crawl before you, don't want to play nice –
I'm perfectly happy to spit in your mugs:
I'm the spendthrift and prodigal of words without price.

·1913·

They Just Don't Get It

Went into the barber's shop, said – calmly:
'Do me a solid and trim my ears'.
The smooth-cheeked barber immediately went spiky;
his jaw hung down till his face looked like a pear.
'Madman!
Buffoon!' –
the words were expelled.
Bad language shuttlecocked: Peep! Pish! Tush!
For a longlonglong time
some head giggled,
plucked from the crowd like an elderly radish.

·1913·

In a Car

'What a delightful evening!'
'She,
(pointing at a girl)
was there last night,
right?'
Heard someone talking on the pavement:
'Post off—
a bump in the road
—ice'.
The city suddenly topsyturvied.
A drunk stamped on hats.
Hoardings gaped in fright.
Spat out
O
and S.
And on the hill
Where it wept darkly
and the city
had clambered shyly,
they swallowed it all:
a fat O,
a disgustingly submissive S.

·1913?·

Vladimir Mayakovsky

A Tragedy in a Prologue, Two Scenes, and an Epilogue

DRAMATIS PERSONAE

Vladimir Mayakovsky (a poet, aged twenty to twenty-five).
His Girlfriend (between fourteen and twenty-one feet tall. She
does not speak).
Old Man with Skinny Black Cats (several thousand years old).
Man with No Eyes or Legs.
Man with No Ears.
Man with No Head.
Man with Stretchy Face.
Man with Two Kisses.
Commonplace Young Man.
Woman with A Little Tear.
Woman with A Standard-Sized Tear.
Woman with A Gigantic Tear.
Paper-boys, Boys, Girls &c.

Prologue

MAYAKOVSKY:
I don't know if you'll get it,
the reason why I
walk through a storm of jeers,
my soul on a platter
offered up for the future to eat.
Like an unnecessary tear
rolling down the cheeks of the squares,
I,
perhaps,
am the last ever poet.
Have you seen
how the striped face of boredom
is hanged in the cobbled lanes,

and how,
into the foam
round the necks of hurrying rivers,
the bridges press their iron hands?
The sky is crying
impetuously,
wild,
and the little cloud
grimaces, a wrinkled pout,
as if it were a woman expecting a child
to whom God had abandoned a crippled idiot.
With its fat fingers covered in reddish hairs,
the sun has stroked you like a gadfly, desperate to sting:
in your souls a slave has been kissed till he collapses.
Fearlessly,
I've carried my hatred of daylight through the years;
with my soul stretched tight as a nervous string,
I
am the king of lamps!
Come unto me,
you who tore through silence
and bellowed
because the midday nooses were tight,
and I will show you,
in language as simple as mooing,
our new souls
humming
like streetlights.
I shall do no more than touch your head, and you will
grow lips
for vast kisses
and a tongue
that can speak all languages.
And I shall go to my throne, a little hobbled soul,
to sit where the stars are holes in the eroded arches.
I will lie down,
shining,

in my raiment of idleness
on a soft bed of genuine crap,
and softly,
kissing the sleepers' knees,
a steam-engine's wheel will caress my nape.

Scene One

*A cheerful scene. We are in a city with its spiderweb of streets. A feast day
for beggars.* MAYAKOVSKY *stands alone. People bring food, the iron
herring from a shop sign, a huge golden pretzel, swags of yellow velvet.*

MAYAKOVSKY:
All you kind people!
Stick a cork in my soul,
so its emptiness can't ooze away.
I don't know if being spat on is an insult or not.
I'm as dry as a graven image.
I've been milked dry.
All you kind people,
do you want
to see me dance for you, a wonderful poet?

Enter the OLD MAN WITH SKINNY BLACK CATS. *He strokes
them. He has an enormous beard.*

MAYAKOVSKY:
Look for the fat ones in their houses like shells
and joyously beat their tambourine bellies!
Catch the deaf and the dumb by their feet
and blow in their ears, like the nostrils of a flute.
Trample out the vintage where the grapes of wrath are stored,
for today I eat the hot cobbles of thought.
Today, as you cry out your toasts, raucous and tawdry,
I shall wear the laurels of my own insanity.

The stage slowly fills up. The MAN WITH NO EARS, *the* MAN WITH
NO HEAD *&c. They are dull and slow. Disorder; they carry on eating.*

MAYAKOVSKY:
In a barefoot jeweller's faceted lines,
the work of one who plumps the feather-beds in other people's
houses,
today I'll light the fuse of a wordwide celebration
for all these bright, rich and beggarly carousers.

OLD MAN WITH CATS:
Stop.
Why these childish rattles for wiser heads than yours?
I am a thousand-year-old old man.
And I can see how, on a cross made of laughter,
for you they have crucified a tormented moan.
Over the town there lay one grief (gigantic)
and a hundred other griefs (littler).
And the candles and lamps in their arguments frantic
have drowned out the dawn's gentle whisper.
The soft moons have no power over us,
the streetlights are both more elegant and more prickly.
In the land of cities they have named themselves our masters,
and soulless things come flying to wipe us away.
And a god who's gone mad looks down from the sky
at the shrieking human horde.
And, eaten away by the dust of the highway,
he runs his hands through his beard.
He's god,
and he screams that your souls are eroding,
he screams that it's time for harsh payback.
Abandon him!
There's cats that need stroking,
go forth and stroke cats that are skinny and black.
Yes, you'll boastfully grasp your belly's spare tire,
you'll puff your smooth cheeks up like pastries.
But it's only in cats
with their raven-sheened fur
that you'll find the sparks of electric eyes.
And the sparks that we gather

(a miraculous draught!)
will pour into a wire, a strong-dragging tendon,
and the trams will start running incredibly fast
and electric flames – victory banners – will shine.
The world will shift, wearing joyful mascara;
each windowbox will be peacocked with flowerets;
the people will travel by rail,
and after
will come cats, cats on cats, cats, cats, cats, cats, black cats!
We'll use the stars to forge silver brooches;
we'll pin the sun to our lover's skirts,
Leave your apartments!
There's cats that need stroking:
skinny ones, black ones, go forth and stroke cats!

MAN WITH NO EARS:
He's right!
Over the city –
where the weathervanes stand on their poles –
a woman
is rushing
and spits down on the pavement
(her eyes are black cavernous holes):
and the gobs where she gobs them grow into cripples.
And somebody's guilt flew overhead now:
the people all gathered,
moved forward as one.
And a little old man cried at the piano –
over there,
on the wallpaper,
near the stains of wine.

They gather round.

MAN WITH NO EARS:
The rumours of torture spread over the city.
If you grab at the music

your fingers will bleed!
But the piano player can't take his hands from the keys,
the white teeth in the mouth of the furious keyboard.

Alarums.

MAN WITH NO EARS:
And since
this
morning,
a cabaret song has planted its lips in my soul.
I was walking along, shaking,
spreading my fingers,
and the chimneys danced on the gables,
cancanning their legs like the number 44!
Gentlemen!
Stop!
Could this really be happening?
The alleys rolled up their sleeves, got ready to rumble.
And my melancholy grows,
incomprehensible and maddening,
like a tear on a sleeping dog's muzzle.

Further alarums

OLD MAN WITH CATS:
You see!
We have to destroy it, carve it all up!
I wasn't wrong to sense the evil in their blandishments!

MAN WITH STRETCHY FACE:
But maybe things just need to be loved?
Maybe things' souls have different constituents?

MAN WITH NO EARS:
Lots of things are inside out.
They are deaf to wickedness,

their hearts know no anger.
MAN WITH STRETCHY FACE (*eagerly nodding*):
And where a normal person has a mouth,
lots of things have got an ear!

MAYAKOVSKY:
Don't stain your hearts' tips with evil!
For you,
my children,
your lessons will be harsh and sharp.
Each of you is nothing but a bell
on God's jester's cap.
On these search-swollen feet
I have walked through this and all adjacent lands
wearing darkness's domino mask.
I looked for her, the soul unseen,
so I could press to my lip-wounds
her healing flowers.

A pause.

MAYAKOVSKY:
And again,
like a slave,
in a bloody sweat,
madness rocks my body.
And I did find her, the soul, she appeared in a blue bonnet,
and said, 'Sit down, I've been waiting for you. Would you like
some tea?'

A pause.

MAYAKOVSKY:
I am a poet,
I've wiped away the differences
between what I look like and how others look.
I have sought my sisters in the morgue's pus

and artfully kissed the sick.
But today
I would throw onto a yellow bonfire –
hiding my tears deeper than plummet did ever sink –
every single sister's pudeur,
every single mother's wrinkles!
We will eat this century like meat, we'll eat our fill,
licking the plates!

They pull back the veil. An enormous woman. Pretty scary. The
COMMONPLACE YOUNG MAN *runs onstage. Commotion.*

MAYAKOVSKY (*aside*):
                    Gentlemen!
They say that somewhere –
maybe in Brazil –
there exists a truly happy man!

COMMONPLACE YOUNG MAN (*running to each person onstage
and kissing them*):
Gentlemen!
Stop!
Gentlemen!
Sirs,
sirs,
tell me at once:
do you really want to burn
mothers?
You, sir!
Man's mind's keen
but it is nothing faced with the world's riddles;
but you want to light a conflagration
using knowledge and books to kindle it!
I've invented a machine for cutting steak.
I'm not any kind of fool!
I know a man who for twenty-five years has tried to make
a flea-catching-tool.

I have a wife,
she'll soon give birth to a son or daughter,
and here you are saying things that are so horrible!
Intelligent people!
You're almost behaving offensively.

MAN WITH NO EARS:
Young fellow,
up on your soapbox!

VOICE FROM THE CROWD:
Or how about a barrel!

MAN WITH NO EARS:
Yeah, no one can see.

COMMONPLACE YOUNG MAN:
It's no laughing matter!
I've got a brother,
a little one,
and you'd come along and chew on his bones.
You'd eat up everything! You'd eat up each other!

Alarums. Sirens. Shouts from offstage: 'Trousers! Trousers!'

MAYAKOVSKY:
Give over!

The COMMONPLACE YOUNG MAN *is surrounded.*

MAYAKOVSKY:
If you had ever been hungry like I've been,
then you would gnaw
on East and West's wide open spaces,
like the bone of heaven is gnawed
by the smoked faces of factories!

COMMONPLACE YOUNG MAN:
What,
are you saying there's nothing of value to love?
I have a sister, her name is Sonia! A sister!

On his knees.

Dear people!
Don't spill any blood!
Gentle people,
no need for a bonfire!

The confusion increases. Shots. A sluicepipe plays a single drawn-out note. The corrugated iron roof starts to wail.

MAN WITH STRETCHY FACE:
If you had ever loved like I have
then you would have murdered her
or else found a place of execution
and from there corrupted the milky-innocent stars,
the hairy sweating heavens.

MAN WITH NO EARS:
Your women don't know how to love,
kisses have swollen them up, like sponges.

The noise of thousands of feet striking the square's taut belly.

MAN WITH STRETCHY FACE:
And they can use my soul as their cloth
to sew such elegant dresses!

The excitement is unconfined. They all gather around the enormous woman. They lift her onto their shoulders, start to move her.

EVERYONE:
We go

to where, for his saintliness,
they crucified a prophet;
we give our bodies over to a naked dance:
we shall raise a monument to red meat
on the black granite of sin and vice.

They drag her to the door. Sound of hurrying steps. The MAN WITH
NO EYES OR LEGS. *Joyful. The madness breaks loose. They drop the*
woman.

MAN WITH NO EYES OR LEGS:
Stop!
Out in the street,
where everyone
seems to be cursed
to wear the same face,
like a burden,
Time, that old woman, has just given birth
to a huge
and grimacing rebellion!
Laughter!
When they saw the faces of the years to come
crawling towards them, the oldsters grew numb,
and anger swelled in the foreheads of towns,
with rivers growing like thousand-mile-long veins.
Slowly,
horrified,
hair like clock hands
rose up on the bald head of Time.
And all things,
their voices cracking,
ran,
abandoning the rags of their threadbare names.
Liquor store displays,
as though pushed by the finger of Satan,
splashed in the bottles' bottom.
Trousers ran away from a tailor who'd fainted

and
walked around –
all by themselves! –
with no thighs to support them.
Drunk –
its black jaws hanging open –
from the bedroom a tallboy stumbled.
Corsets clambered down, scared of falling,
from the signs reading '*Robes et modes*'.
The playful winking
of stocking-coquettes.
Every single galosh was haughty and strict.
I ran fast as a curse.
My other leg's
still over there in the next street.
What do you mean when you shout that
I'm a cripple,
you old
fat,
bloated foes,
you dregs?
If you search the whole world now
you won't stumble
over a single man
with a
matching pair
of legs!

Curtain

Scene Two

Boring. A square in the new town. MAYAKOVSKY *is now wearing a toga. Laurel wreath. Lots of legs visible behind the door.*

MAN WITH NO EYES OR LEGS (*servilely*):
Poet!
Poet!

They've declared you a prince.
Your subjects
are crowding outside,
sucking their fingers.
And on the ground in front of them everyone has
some kind of ridiculous container.

MAYAKOVSKY:
Well then,
let them enter!

Timidly. THREE WOMEN *carrying jars. A lot of bowing.*

WOMAN WITH A LITTLE TEAR:
Here's my little tear:
take it!
It's not something I need.
Here you go.
Here it is,
white,
made from the silk
eyes release in grief.

MAYAKOVSKY (*worried*):
I don't need it,
why me?
(*addressing the next woman*)
Are your eyes puffed up from crying?

WOMAN WITH A STANDARD-SIZED TEAR (*carelessly*):
Fiddle-de-dee!
My son's dying.
It's nothing serious.
Here's another tear.
It would make a lovely buckle.
You could put it on your slipper.

MAYAKOVSKY *is frightened.*
WOMAN WITH A GIGANTIC TEAR:
Yes, I know,
I'm a mess,
don't pay it any mind.
I'll have a wash,
get cleaner.
Here's my tear for you,
ain't she fine?
A really gigantic tear.

MAYAKOVSKY:
Got enough.
Must be off.
Who's that delightful young lady?

PAPER-BOYS:
Telegraph!
Telegraph!
Times, Standard, Guardian, Indie!

The MAN WITH TWO KISSES *enters. Everyone looks round. They speak in fits and starts.*

EVERYONE:
Look at him –
how wild he looks!
Step back a bit.
It's dark.
Let me through!
Young man,
don't hiccup!

MAN WITH NO HEAD:
Ee-ee-ee-ee…
Eh-eh-eh-eh…

MAN WITH TWO KISSES:
The clouds are yielding to the sky,
loose-skinned and ugly.
Day's gone smash.
The girls of the air will give it out for money,
they only want cash.

MAYAKOVSKY:
What?

MAN WITH TWO KISSES:
Cash, I'm telling you, cash!

VOICES:
Shush!
Shush!

MAN WITH TWO KISSES (*doing a dance, juggling balls filled
with holes*):
This large and dirty man
had two kisses given to him.
He was an awkward man,
he didn't know
what to do with them,
where to go.
The town,
on holiday,
in the cathedrals raised up hallelujahs,
and people were dressed in their finest clothes.
But this man was cold,
and there were oval holes in his soles.
He took the bigger kiss
and put it on like a galosh.
But the cold was intense,
and his fingers all froze.
'What the hell,'
the man said angrily,

'these useless kisses are going in the trash.'
And he threw them away,
but suddenly
one of the kisses grew ears,
and started to wriggle,
then in a thin voice it shouted
'Mum!'
The man was wracked by fears.
He wrapped the shivering body in the rags of his soul, and
                                        carried it home.

The man rifled through dusty suitcases
(looking for a frame to put the kiss in).
He looked up, and the kiss
was lying on the divan,
huge,
fat,
all grown up,
laughing,
raging!
'Lord!'
the man wept.
'I'd never have thought I'd be so tired.
Time for me to hang!'
And while he hung there,
ugly,
and pitiful –
in their boudoirs, women
(smoke-free, chimneyless workshops),
manufactured billions of kisses
of all kinds,
big
and small,
with the fleshy levers of their lips.

AN IRRUPTION OF CHILD-KISSES (*rapidly*):
They've set a lot of us free.
Grab the ones you can!

The rest will be along soon,
for the time being we're just eight.
I'm
Ivan.
Go ahead!

Each one lays down a tear.

MAYAKOVSKY:
Gentlemen!
Listen:
I can't do this!
You're all fine,
but what about my agonies?

THREATS:
You carry on with what you're doing!
We'll grind your bones to make our bread!

OLD MAN WITH ONE SHAVEN CAT:
You're the only one who can sing.

Points at the heap of tears.

Take these to your red godhead.

MAYAKOVSKY:
Let me sit down!

They don't let him sit down. MAYAKOVSKY *hesitates awkwardly, gathers the tears into a suitcase. He stands holding the suitcase.*

Alright,
make way!
Only joy, no need for regret.
With shining eyes
I'll sit on the throne,

a Greek in my epicene body.
No!
The northern rivers' grey hair
I will never forget,
or the thin legs of the roadways.
And today,
I will go out through the city,
leaving my soul
on the houses' spears,
scrap after scrap.
And the moon
to the breach in the heavens
will travel with me.
Then come up beside me
and try on my hat.
I will walk
shouldering my burden,
stumbling,
crawling,
into the north,
to that place where,
with the fingers of waves,
the monstrous ocean
constantly tears at its breast
in the grip of endless grief.
Shattered, I will force myself there.
This will be the end.
I will howl.
I will rave.
And to the dark god of storms
I will offer each tear,
at the wellspring of bestial faiths.

Curtain

Epilogue

MAYAKOVSKY:
I wrote all this
about you,
poor rats.
I was sad I had no breasts,
or I'd have fed you all like a kind wet-nurse.
But now I'm dried up
(wrinkled dugs, drained sacks),
and a little bit delirious.
But
who else
and where else
would have given his thoughts such inhuman freedom?
I pulled back the curtain in Oz,
proved that the Man Upstairs is a scam.
Sometimes I think:
I'm a Dutch cockerel,
or else:
I'm a king of the Pskov dynasty.
But sometimes I like
my own name best of all:
Vladimir Mayakovsky.

·1913·

War Is Declared

'Read all about it! Extra! Extra!
Italy! Austria! Germany!'
And on the black-bordered city square
crimson blood poured out in streams!

The coffee shop beat a face to a pulp,
purpled it with its wild cry:
'With the thunder of cannon we'll poison Rome's marble;
we'll poison with blood the waves of the Rhine!'

From the sky, torn by the stings of bayonets,
the star-tears sifted down, like flour through a sieve,
and desire trodden flat by bootsoles screamed out:
'Let me live, let me live, let me live, let me live!'

The bronze generals on their faceted plinths
cried out: 'Set us free, and we'll march to the war!'
The cavalry said goodbye with a clip-clop kiss,
and the infantry yearned for victory-murder.

There was born, in a dream, to the piled-up town,
the laughing bass voice of a cannon;
and from the west falls crimson snow
in juicy flakes of shredded human.

Squadron after squadron swells up on the square;
the veins stand out on the furious forehead.
'The cocotte's silk dress is where we'll wipe our sabres;
we'll wipe them on the Viennese boulevards!'

The newspapers exploded: 'Read all about it!
Austria! Germany! Italy!'
And from the firmly black-bordered night
the crimson blood poured and poured in streams.

· 20 July 1914 ·

Mother and the Evening the Germans Killed

Along the black streets white mothers cried,
and shudderingly stretched themselves, like funeral brocade.
They cried among those who exulted over the beaten enemies:
'Shut, oh shut the newspaper's eyes!'

A letter.

Mother, louder!
Smoke.
Smoke.
More smoke!
What are you mumbling, mother, to me?
Be aware –
The air is thick
With stones that groan under the attacking artillery.
Mo-o-o-th-e-e-er!
They've just dragged in a wounded evening.
He held on for a long time,
shaggy-haired,
his tail docked,
but suddenly –
his cloudy shoulders started heaving,
and he burst into tears, poor mite, on Warsaw's neck.
The stars in their dark blue calico kerchiefs
screamed:
'He's been killed,
oh dear one,
my dear one!'
And the cross-eyed eye of the new moon glommed
to the dead fist clutching the rifle's magazine.
Lithuanian villages came running to see
how Kaunas, forged into a stump by a kiss,
twisted its finger-streets,
with tears in the churches' golden eyes.
But the evening cried out,

with no legs
and no arms,
'It's just a flesh wound,
I can still, if you please –
ha, ha! –
twirl my blond moustache
as I dance a fiery mazurka, clinking my spurs!'

A ring at the door.

What is it,
mother?
White, white as funeral linen.
'Don't touch me, please!
This is about him,
a telegram, about the dead man.
Shut,
oh shut the newspaper's eyes!'

·1914·

Cloud in Trousers

A Tetraptych

Your thoughts
loll about your brainmush like a fat
lackey on a greasy divan –
I'll stir them up with the bloody scraps of my heart;
I'll over-insult you, I'll be brazen.

There's not a single grey hair on my soul,
and in it no old man's tenderness.
I walk along – handsome, twenty-two years old,
I threaten the world
with my powerful voice.

Gentle people!
You play love on a violin.
A crude man bangs it out on the timpani.
But just like me, none of you can turn
yourselves inside-out to be lip and lip only!

Come here and study –
come away from your chintzy
three-piece suite, you angelic bureaucrat.

You who pore over those lips so peacefully,
like a cook who browses her Mrs Beeton.

If you want,
I'll be made of rampant flesh,
or else – like the sun comes back after showers –
if you want,
I'll be impeccably light of touch,
not a man, but a cloud in trousers!

This won't be some romp on the Côte d'Azur!
No, the people I will extol are men,
who lie about idle as a hospital ward,
and also, tired as cliché, women.

1.

You think this is delirium, the babbling of malaria?

This happened,
in Odessa it happened.

'I'll come by at four,' said Maria.

Eight o'clock.
Nine.
Ten.

The evening
drew back from the windows,
afraid of the dark,
gloomy,
like December.

There! Laughing at me behind my decrepit back –
the candelabras.

Recognise me? No you wouldn't:
a vast gangly thing
that groans
and scrunches up.
What could such a clod want?
But a clod can want so much!

The clod doesn't care
that it's made out of bronze,

that its heart is as cold as iron.
At night it wants to hide its groans
in something soft,
in something like a woman.

And here
I hunch,
huge at the window –
with my forehead I melt the window-pane.
So, will there be love or no?
What sort of a love –
tiny or grand?
How could a large love come out of this:
it has to be a small one,
a submissive lovelet.
It likes the sound of horses'
hooves, is startled to hear cars hoot.

The rain falls, I am jostled by it –
my face is pressed against its pock-marked face
over and over.
I wait,
spattered by the town's shoreline thunder.

Midnight comes with a knife,
catching up,
cutting –
that's it!

This is the stroke of twelve,
the stroke that severs the condemned man's head.

Grey raindrops screech down
the window and distort my face,
as the gargoyles might howl
on Notre-Dame of Paris.

Damn her!
What does she want, if this isn't enough?
Soon a scream will tear my mouth to pieces.

Listen:
quietly,
a nerve
has jumped up
like a sick man from his bed.
This is
how it starts, slowly at first
and then running,
worried
and distinct.
Now this nerve and two others
Start to tapdance, frantic.

On the floor below the plaster's coming down.

Nerves –
big ones,
small ones,
a whole bunch of nerves! –
they clip-clop madly, even now
their legs are starting to give!

And the night in the room gets murkier and marshier –
a heavy eye couldn't drag itself out of here.

The doors suddenly flutter –
like in a hotel,
they don't fit quite square.

You came in,
as sharp as 'screw you!',
playing with your gloves, distracted,
you said:

'listen –
I'm getting married.'

Well then.
Nothing to say.
I'll live. Get out.
Look how calm I am!
Like the heartbeat
of a dead man.

Do you remember?
You said:
'The call of the wild,
money,
passion,
love,'
and only I saw
you had a Mona Lisa smile
somebody had to grab hold of!

And you were grabbed.

I should just get
out there again –
my furrowed brow lit with love's fire.
Why not!
Even a burnt-out
house sometimes gets squatters!

Are you making fun of me?
'Not at all, I'm not adding a penny
to your imaginings, your wealth of madness.'
Just be careful!
Remember what happened to Pompeii
when she made fun of Vesuvius!

Hey!
Gentlemen!
You lovers of sacrilege,
warfare,
crime –
here's the most terrible thing
you've ever seen –
my
face when
I
am absolutely calm.

And I feel that
'I'
is not enough for me.
Something tears itself away, something stubborn.

Hello!
'Hello, who's speaking, please?'
Hello?
Mother?
Mother!
Your son is seriously ill.
Mother!
His heart is on fire.
Tell his sisters, tell Liuda and Olya
there's nothing that can be done to help any more.
Every word,
even the jokes
that burp out of his burning mouth,
throw themselves out, like prostitutes jumping naked
from a blazing brothel.

People sniff the air –
something's burning!
And now others rush past.
Shiny!

Wearing helmets!
No time to get their boots on!
Tell the firemen to caress themselves into this heart.

And here I am.
My eyes pour out barrelfuls of tears.
Lean against my ribcage, here.
I'm going to jump! I'm going to jump! Here I come!
Crash.
Don't jump out of your own heart!

On the burned-out face,
from the lip-fissure,
a little kiss prepares to throw itself down, quite charred.

I can't sing,
mother.
There was a choir in the church of my heart!

Like children from a burning building –
out of my skull
come words and numbers, their burnt remains.
This is how fear,
grasping at the sky,
spread out
the burning hands of the *Lusitania*.

Fresh from the docks,
jolting into
the quiet flat
a hundred-eyed dawn pokes us with its rays.
Make it last for a century, this final shout –
to tell the world that I'm ablaze!

2.

Glory to me!
The great are no match for me.
On everything ever made
I set my stamp: 'rejected'.
I never need ever to read.
Books?
What are books?

I once suspected
that books came about
like this: here comes a poet –
he unclips
his mouth – the inspired fool blurts something out
and Bob's your uncle!
But before he starts to sing,
it seems that
he has to walk a long way,
get callused, and quietly guddle the stupid trout
of inspiration in his heart's slimy waterways.
And as he boils away, scraping at his rhymes,
stewing together love and nightingales,
the street outside breathlessly writhes –
it has nothing with which it can chatter or call.
The towns' Babel towers
lift themselves proud
but god
strikes the towns
down to the ground,
and muddles their words.

The street silently goes through torment.
A scream stands straight up in every gullet.
Puffy taxis and bony hansoms
bristle, stuck through the throat.
People are out of breath,

as if struck with TB.

The town barricades the road with darkness.

And then –
the street pushes a church out the way
and onto the square a crowd flobs.
The poet thinks:
'god will feel I've humbled
him, and come with whip and knout!'
But the bored street sits there and grumbles:
'let's go get some takeout!'

Wayne and Waynetta paint the town red,
pucker neanderthal brows –
but in their gob
the little corpses of most words lie dead.
Only two pull through:
'wanker'
and 'kebab'.

Soaked through with tears,
the sodden poets
ran away from the street, blowing their noses:
'how can we sing to people like that
about strawberries,
maidens,
lilac and roses?'

But, following the poets
thousands come from the street:
students,
prostitutes,
builders.
Gentlemen, ladies and gentlemen!
Whoa there! Wait!
You can't ask for crumbs,

you aren't beggars!

We are the healthy ones –
each stride six feet long,
we mustn't listen to these people, but
tear them apart, these poets who cling on
for free to every double bed!

Don't ask them humbly
to help you, don't pray for hymns or fine oratorios!
We are the creators of our own blazing hymnbook –
the noise from the factories and the laboratories!

What's *Faust* to me –
a dainty rocket
that squeezes up to the sky along with Mephistopheles!
When there's a nail sticking into my boot,
it's more nightmarish than all Goethe's fantasy!

My
mouth is golden,
my words and figments
make your body happy,
rejuvenate your soul:
and I say unto you:
the smallest fragment
of life is more than all I have done
or ever will!

Listen up!
Some modern loudmouth sermonises,
threatening and moaning –
a real Zarathustra!
We,
with our slept-on, rumpled faces,
with lips that hang down like a chandelier,
we,

prisoners in this colony of vice,
where gold and dirt are both tainted with leprosy –
we are cleaner than any lagoon in Venice,
washed by the sea and the sun permanently!

Who gives a toss
that in Homer or Ovid
there's no one like us,
covered in soot?
I know that the sun would go dark if it
just once saw the seams of gold in our spirit!

This is the true prayer – muscles and veins.
Shall we suck all the charity out of this time?
Every one of us
has the reins
to guide the world lying in his palm!

Golgotha took place again
in the auditoria of Petrograd, Odessa, Kiev, Moscow,
and there wasn't anyone
who wouldn't shout, 'crucify him, crucify him now!'
But
all you people
who insulted me
are closer than ever to me, even sweeter.

Haven't you seen
how a dog will lick the hand that beats it?

I am
laughed at by the people of today
like a big fat dirty joke,
but I see something that nobody
else sees –
someone coming across time's mountain-peaks.

Over there, where the normal gaze falls short,
comes the year 1916
tramping at the head of a starving horde,
wearing revolution's thorny crown.

To this, I am sent to bear
witness; where there is pain, I am there;
I crucify myself over and over
in every falling tear.
Already there is nothing left to ask for.
Where mercy once grew, I have inflamed souls.
This is hard, harder, much, much harder
than capturing a million Bastilles!

And when
his arrival
resounds with mutiny,
come to your saviour –
I will pull out your soul, hammer it flat, hand it back to you –
bloody, like a banner.

3.

Why oh why
is my bright happiness
attacked by these threatening gestures,
by these clenched fists?
Thoughts of the madhouse; my head hangs in despair.

And –
as crewmen jump through
the hatches of a dreadnought that tears itself to pieces –
through my gaping eyes,
opened wide enough to scream through,
David Burliuk* clambered in a panic, crazy.
He crawled from under my cried-out

almost bloodstained eyelids,
pulled himself together,
stood,
and with a tenderness unexpected in one so fat
took me up and said,
 'good!'

Good, is it,
when you wrap your heart in a yellow
waistcoat to try
and keep your fellows'
mocking eyes away?

Good,
when in return for a solid
lump-sum to his bereaved family
the condemned man shouts to the crowd at the scaffold,
'Buy all your chocolate from Cadbury!'?

But that moment –
rowdy,
exotic –
I wouldn't exchange it for anything,
not anything…

But then, from the cigar smoke
and the snifter, sticks the drunk face of Severyanin.[†]

How dare he call himself
a poet? He croons like a quail and he has grey hair.

---

[*] David Burliuk (1882–1967), Russian Futurist artist and poet, the first person to take Mayakovsky's poetry seriously.

[†] Igor Severyanin ('Igor the Northerner', penname of the Russian decadent poet Igor Vasilievich Lotaryov (1887–1941) whose pseudo-Futurism concealed a strong conservative streak.

Nowadays
the world needs
tough love:
a going-over with a knuckleduster!

Oh you pretty things,
you people
who only worry about looking good when you dance,
look at me instead, a green baize card-sharp –
how do I relax, a vulgar ponce…

I walk away from you all,
who have been soaked by love,
who poured out your tears for a century,
and I put the sun as a monocle
into my wide-open eye.

I dress myself up fantastically,
and go around,
trying to please
people and fire them up,
and before me goes Napoleon on a leash,
just like a pug.

Like a woman, the whole world lies back,
fidgets
with her flesh, wants to give herself to me;
things start to revive,
their lips
lisp out,
'come here, come on, big boy'.

Suddenly,
all the clouds boil
frantically up, like
white workmen downing tools,
telling the sky that they've gone on strike.

Thunder climbed brutally out of the storm clouds –
huge nostrils cleared with vigour,
the sky twisted its face for a second
into the strict grimace of Bismarck.

And somebody, having lost his way
in the clouds, held out his hand
towards the café –
like a woman perhaps,
gently perhaps,
perhaps like a gun.

Do you think that it's the kind sun
that pinches the cheeks of the café?
It is General Gallifet, marching off again
to shoot down another mutiny.

Passerby, take your hands out of your pants –
pick up a stone or a knife or a bomb,
and if you don't happen to have any hands
butt your foe with your head or kick him!

O come all ye hungry,
ye submissive,
ye sweaty,
ye apathetic in yr flea-bitten duds.

Come along! We'll make
Mondays and Tuesdays holidays,
we'll paint them bright with blood.
As the earth comes under the knife,
let it remember
whom it wanted to vulgarise (the earth, itself
as flabby as one of Rothschild's lovers!).

Let the flags fly in the heat of the cannonade,
as if it were any normal holiday –

and you, lampposts, stand up straight,
put the hanged carcases on display.

I was all argued-out,
I'd begged enough,
I spoke plainly,
I went to buttonhole someone else.

The sunset quivered in the sky,
dying, red as the Marseillaise.

This is madness already.

Nothing's going to happen.

Night will come,
have a drink or two,
sit down to dinner.

Do you see –
the sky is Judas once again,
clutching in his hand a few treacherous stars.

Night's here.
It feasts like an ogre
and settles its arse on the city tenements.
You can't see anything,
it's so obscure –
as vague and black as a double-agent.

I run away to a pub to hide,
I cover the tablecloth and my soul with wine
and I see
in the corner – my eyes go wide –
looking deep into my heart, the Virgin.

What, to the bright young things in this bar,
can a painted icon offer?
You see, once again
it's Barabbas they prefer
to the spurned man of Golgotha.

Maybe I'm here on purpose,
in this human mash
where nobody's face is new.
Of all your sons,
it is I,
perhaps,
who am the most beautiful.

Let them die off soon,
the older generation,
mouldy with happiness –
we need to grow up:
let those who are now just kids have children –
boys become fathers,
girls get knocked up.

And let there be on the shoulders of these children
old, learned, respectable bald heads,
and let them
come unto me, and let them be christened
with the names
of my poems.

I sing the motorcar and England:
in this most ordinary of gospels,
I may be –
do you understand? –
the thirteenth apostle.

And as my voice
obscenely yells

from hour to hour,
for whole
days on end, maybe Jesus Christ will smell
the forget-me-nots of my soul.

4.

Maria! Maria! Maria!
Let me in, Maria! I can't
stay out on the street!
You don't want
to? Just you wait!
Wait until your cheeks collapse into dimples
that everyone has had, wait till your taste has faded away –
I will come by and toothlessly mumble
that I am 'exceptionally honest' with you today.

Look, Maria, I've already started to stoop.

I see people opening the windows in their four-storey goitres –
they hang their eyes out and laugh at me,
because I have –
once again! –
the crust of yesterday's
caresses clamped in my teeth.

The rain sobbed onto the pavement in pools,
it went at the cobblestones
like a tiny pickpocket rifling a corpse,
but from the grey eyelashes,
from the icicles
fell tears –
yes, tears! –
from the downcast eyes of the drainpipes.
The rain sucked the faces off all the passersby
and a reflection sat next to the real man

in the coach windows:
pig fat oozed out
when the people split their sides;
as well as the sodden crust,
an old porkchop floated down the road.

Maria!
How can I slip a quiet word in at the window?
A bird begs with songs,
it sings hungry and loudly,
but I am a person, Maria,
simply that –
the consumptive night coughed me up into Moscow's dirty hand.
Is this what you want?
Maria, let me in.
Maria!
I grasp the doorknocker by its iron throat.

Maria!
The streets are running wild.
The crowd scratches my cheek with its fingers.

Open up!

It hurts!

Look, I've been spiked in the eye
with a hat-pin!

She opened up.

Dearest!
Don't be scared
of this other
woman who hugs tight to my neck, smelling of animal-sweat and
                                        wet with grief –
it is my fate to drag

a million huge clean love-monsters
and a billion little lovelets with me through life.

Don't be scared
that once again
in a foul-weather excess
I will snuggle up to a thousand pretty faces –
'Mayakovsky's exes!' –
they're just ghosts –
a dynasty of deposed princesses.

Maria, come closer!

I won't make you tremble naked before me,
just give me the matchless charm of your lips:
my heart has never grown up as far as May,
but a full life holds at least a hundred Aprils.

Maria!
A poet is happiest when he's writing,
but I'm a man,
I'm made of flesh and blood –
I'm asking for your body,
asking like a Christian:
'give me this day my daily bread'.

Maria, give it to me!

Maria, I'm scared of forgetting your name,
like a poet fears
losing the perfect words,
born at midnight in his bed.
I will care for your body and love it, like a wounded soldier,
an unnecessary man,
a nobody,
cares for his remaining leg.

Maria –
you don't want to?
You don't want to!

Ha!

Well, dark and downcast,
I'll take up my heart once again
and carry it off
crying
like a dog carries his paw
back to the kennel,
after it's been cut off by a train.

My heart's blood will make the road happy,
the red flowers show bright among the dust
on my coat. Like the sun round the earth, a thousand times
                                              Salome
will dance round the head of the Baptist.

And when my tally of years
finally plays itself out
a million drops of blood will cover
the road to my father's house.

I'll climb up to heaven –
I'll be dirty (I slept in the gutter).
I'll stand next to him, bend down
and speak into his ear:

'Listen up, mister god!
Don't you get bored up here in the sky,
spending all day looking down?
Here's a plan – let's chop down that tree
(the one in your garden…) and make it into a merry-go-round!

'If you're omnipresent, you can get into all
the cellars and bring some quality wine back up –

then maybe, just maybe, Peter the Apostle
can be persuaded to lighten up.
And let's get some Eves back among the heavenly host:
I'll show you –
this evening I'll gather the most
beautiful girls from the boulevards for you.

'You want to?

'You don't want to?
Do you shake your head,
goldilocks? Are you frowning? Do you think that all this…
all this wingèd
nonsense here has a clue about what love is?

'I'm also an angel, I was one back down there –
I looked out through these eyes like a little
lamb. But I'm wasting my sweetness on the desert air:
it's like setting up a china shop and whistling for a bull!
You're omnipotent, and you thought up hands
and you gave everybody a head,
or something –
how come you couldn't work out a plan
so we could kiss, kiss, kiss without suffering?

'I thought you were all-powerful, the real god-almighty,
but you're just a dimwit, a crusty little godkin.
See, I bend down,
and from the top of my
boot, pull out my shiv, my bare bodkin.
You scoundrel, you with your wings!
It's only in heaven you have any presence!
You must be scared – your feathers are bristling!
I'll slice you from here to Alaska, you and your incense!

'Goodbye!'
They can't stop me.

I may be right or wrong, but I can't settle down.
Look – they've got blood all over the sky
and they've beheaded the stars again.

Hey you!
Sky!
Take off your hat! Can't you see
I'm coming?

Needs to wash out its ears.

The universe is asleep,
and one huge ear –
covered in stars like fleas –
flops over its paws.

· 1914–15 ·

I and Napoleon

I live on Bolshaya Presnya,
36, 24.
A peaceful spot.
Calm.
Yeah,
and I'm like, what business is it of mine
if somewhere
in the whole wide world
people have thought they should have a war?

Night fell.
Pleasant.
Insinuating.
And why do these gentlemen shudder a bit,
with their eyes, worriedly rolling,

as large as floodlights?
The crowds in the street bring their burning lips
towards the heavenly dampness,
and the city, enduring the flags that slap,
prays and prays with red crosses.
A bare-headed little church fell to the boulevard's bedstead –
beaten down by tears –
and blood flows from the boulevard flowerbeds,
like a heart torn by bullets' fingers.
Fatter and fatter grows anxiety,
as it takes stale reason and chews and chews.
Already Noah's orangeries
are covered in deadly white gauze!
Tell Moscow –
hold tight! Hang on!
No need!
It mustn't falter, it mustn't!
In a second
I'll meet
the dictator of heaven,
I'll up and kill the sun!
You see him!
Flags shake in the air.
There he is!
Fat and ginger, with his red hoof.
He stamps it crashing against the square
as he enters over the corpses of roofs!

To you,
the one who screams
'I will destroy,
I will destroy!',
gutting the night out of bloody buildings,
I,
putting my dauntless soul on the line,
I throw out a challenge!

Go, you corroded insomnia,
Carry on throwing souls to the fiery pits!
None of this, none of this matters!
Today's last sun's
the sun of Austerlitz!

Go on, you madmen, leave Poland and Russia.
Today I am Napoleon!
I am the general, and even greater.
There's really no comparison!

Just once he brought his court into a plague-zone,
with his bravery teasing death –
Every day, I go to the plague-stricken
through thousands of Russian Jaffas!
Just once, without trembling, he faced the bullets
and now everyone praises his balls...
And I, in one single July
lived through a thousand Arcoles!
You hear that thunder? The cry that comes from my lips.
It will pass through time's granite
because
in my heart, pillaged like Egypt,
there are thousands upon thousands of pyramids!

Get thee behind me, rotting insomnia!
Away to the fiery pits!
And hello to my pre-mortem sun, hello there!
The sun of Austerlitz!

There will be!
People!
On the sun!
Soon!
The sun breaks apart!
Loud from a cathedral's crushed throat: a groan,
a groan, a funeral march!

People!
When they come to memorialise
the dead, more famous than I,
remember:
the war took another life –
the poet from Bolshaya Presnya!

·1915·

You!

You, as from orgy to orgy you stagger –
you, with your heated toilets and private bathrooms! –
aren't you ashamed to flick through the newspaper
and see the list of military decorations?

Did you know, you talentless flock –
thinking about how best to stuff yourself –
that perhaps just now a bomb has taken
the legs of some Lieutenant Petrov?

And what if he, torn to bloody strips,
given over for liquidation,
could see how you with your chop-chomping lips
warble the poems of Severyanin?

To give a life for you and yours,
you lovers of partridge and the pink trombone?
I'd rather be barman to a barful of whores,
serving them pineapple champagne!

·1915·

And That's How I Became a Dog

Well, that's a fucker and no mistake!
I'm so angry it's tearing me apart.
I'm not angry like *you* might be angry:
instead, like a dog I'd make a seizing bite
at the bald moon,
and shred it with my cries.

My nerves are bad tonight...
I'll go out
for a stroll.
Out on the street I didn't calm down, not even a smidgen.
Someone shouted something along the lines of 'good evening'.
And I had to reply,
because I knew this someone.
I want to.
Yet I feel
I couldn't reply in fluent Human.

Madness! How's that for a scandal!
Am I perhaps asleep?
I patted myself –
just the same as I've always been,
the same face I'm used to... the same face... or...?
I touch my mouth
and there, jutting down almost to my chin:
an incisor.

Hands over my face, as though I were blowing my nose.
Loping, I hurried home.
But... as I rounded the police box, trying to keep a low profile,
a deafening scream:
'Officer! He's got a tail!'

I reached thither my hand and – pillar of salt time! –
there it was,

plainer than the muzzle on my face,
and I hadn't even noticed it on my headlong rush:
from underneath my Afghan coat
there fanned a tail, enormous,
curling behind me,
unutterably doggish.

What now?
Someone was yelling; a crowd started to form.
Two people, then three, four: the group began to swell.
They crushed some old dame.
And she, crossing herself, shouted something about the Devil.

And when – their hackles raised, their bathhouse-brush-beards
up in my face – the crowd fell on me, huge and rough,
I went down to the ground on all fours
and started barking: Woof! Woof! Woof!

·1915·

Hey!

Wet, like someone had been licking it,
a crowd.
A mouldy wind blows mustily.
Hey!
Russia,
is it really not allowed,
the slightest hint of novelty?

Blessed is he who might instead –
perhaps by closing his eyes – forget you:
unnecessary as a cold in the head;
sober
as water from San Pellegrino.

You're all so boring, it's as if Capri
didn't have its place in the universe.
But Capri does exist.
The auroras of all the flowery
islands, like a woman in a pink headdress.

Let's take a train to the seaside and leave the seaside
behind us, our bodies swaying on the decks of steamships.
We'll discover America a dozen times.
We'll visit the earth's unknown poles for daytrips.

And look at how gentle-fingered you are,
and as for me –
my hand's so rough.
But perhaps, out of all the swordfighters
in tournaments or duels,
I would be the most skilful.

It's great, when the right hook hits home – a knockout! –
to see how the legs turn to jelly.
Or when logic finds the weak spot
for her sword, in your opponent's ancestry.

And then, in the golden hall's firelight,
unaware of any need for repose,
to stay awake throughout the night
staring
into your cognac's yellow eyes.

And finally, to come out in the morning with a hangover
bristling like a hedgehog, thorny,
and threaten your unfaithful lover
that you'll kill her and throw her corpse into the sea.

Let's abandon this nonsense of jackets and cuffs:
we'll paint starched shirtfronts to look like armour,
we'll grip the handle of a butter knife
and, just for one day, we'll be Spaniards.

I wish that we, forgetting our northern mind,
could fall in love, fight, feel any kind of elation.
Hey!
Man,
invite the earth herself
to come and dance the Charleston!

Think up new stars and put them in the sky;
arise, and lift the sky to the heights again,
and maybe, scrabbling up from the rooftree,
artists will hoick their souls into heaven.

·1916·

To Lily, Instead of a Letter

Tobacco smoke ate up the air.
This room
is a chapter from a Futurist's hellish vision.
And it was just outside that window,
remember,
where I first
passionately stroked your hands.
Your heart dressed in iron,
you sit here today.
One more day
and you'll throw me out,
perhaps scolding me as I leave.
It will take a long time in the dim lobby
for my ticcing arm to worm into my jacket sleeve.
I'll run out,
I'll throw my body into the street.
Wild,
mad,
carved up by despair.

My dearest,
my darling,
this we don't need –
let us now say goodbye to one another.
But
my heavy love –
a dumbbell –
weighs on you
no matter where you run.
Let me give out in one final bellow
the bitterness of my offended complaints.
Say they work an ox until it's tired to death:
he walks off
and slumps in the cool waters.
I
have no sea
apart from your love
and can't beg a holiday there with my tears.
If it's peace an exhausted elephant wants to have,
he will find some hot sand and luxuriantly lie down.
I
have no sun
apart from your love
and I do not know where you are, or with which other man.
If you tortured a poet this way
he'd throw over his lover for money or fame:
but for me
there is nothing that brings me joy
apart from your name, apart from your name.
And I won't drink poison, and I won't throw myself down stairs,
and I won't put a gun to my temple and pull the trigger.
Nothing hangs over me,
apart from your eyes:
no sword of Damocles, no straight-edged razor.
Tomorrow you'll forget
you've been made immortal,
that some blossoming love set this soul aflame,

and the empty days in their whirling carnival
will take up my books and riffle their pages…
My words. Will their dry leaves
make people stop,
make their heart skip a beat?

As a last tenderness,
let me at least
lay them down for your passing feet.

Petrograd

· 26 May 1916 ·

I'm Bored

I can't stay home. Annensky.
Tyutchev. Frickin' Fet.
Driven out to the world by my ennui
I go
to the flicks, to the pubs, to cafés.

At the table.
A brainwave.
Hope brightens this fool's heart.
And what if in a week's time
that Russian there were so changed
that I could light his cheeks with my lips' fire?

I carefully raise my eyes,
peer around the jacketed crowd.
'Run away,
run away,
run away!'

my fearful heart says.
Fear runs over my face, hopeless and bored.

I don't listen to myself.
I see,
a little way off to the right,
diligently working away at a shank of veal,
a mysterious creature of a type
unknown on land or in the depths of the sea.

Does he exist or doesn't he? You look at him and you don't know.
You look at him and you don't know: is he breathing or not?
A couple of yards of faceless pink dough:
if only there were a label sewn on at some spot.

The only thing about him that moves
is the soft folds of his shiny jowls that hang down to his
shoulders.
My heart in a panic
rants and raves.
'Run away!
What are you waiting for?'

I look to the left.
My jaw dropped out of place.
I turned back to the first one, and he'd changed, changed utterly:
by comparison with this second guy, the first guy's face
was a missing masterpiece by Leonardo da Vinci.

People no longer exist.
Can you make sense
of a cry born from three years' torment?
Your soul doesn't want to walk in silence,
but who is there to talk to?

I throw myself down to the ground:
washing the asphalt with my tears,

I rasp my face bloody on the stony crust.
And now – over a tram's intelligent face – a thousand kisses I smear
With my lips exhausted by lust.

I go home.
I stick myself to the rose-patterned wallpaper.
And where are there softer and tea-ier blooms?
Would you like me
to read you *A Cloud in Trousers*
or some of my adolescent poems?

A NOTE FOR HISTORIANS

When everything's divvied up between hell and heaven,
the balance sheet of the earth will be made out.
Remember this:
in 1916,
all the beautiful people vanished from Petrograd.

·1916·

Going Cheap

If I stop a girl in the street and try talking my way
into a sweet romance,
she grabs her purse. Same if I look at normal passersby.
Fools! Who needs to steal cash from a tramp?

How long will it take before they catch on,
these candidates for the city morgue,
that I
am infinitely richer
than any Pierpont Morgan?

A long way into the future, a very long way

(put it like this, I'll be dead and gone,
whether from hunger, or blasting myself away),
professors will study this circus clown,
i.e. me, down to the last tittle and jot.
And some emeritus egghead eggshell
will try to establish what I did and where I did it,
will write papers on *Mayakovsky: God, Myth or Devil?*

He'll judge me without knowing me face to face;
and a servile crowd will fuss and fawn,
and on my balding head they'll place
either a halo or a pair of horns.

But every female student, as she lies in bed reading,
won't escape my poems' excitement:
I may be a pessimist, but – fingers crossed; I'm pleading –
there will always be female students.

Now listen:

I will give you the wealth of my soul –
wealth uncountable, beyond all accountability –
and the magnificence which makes my deeds eternal,
and my own immortality
which, thundering throughout countless aeons,
will push to their knees all the people of the world –
all of this – do you want it? – I will abandon
for one single tender human word.

People!

Raise dust from the avenues, trample the rye,
come from all corners of the earth.
Today in Petrograd, in Hope Street, *chez* Mayakovsky,
a treasure will be sold for far less than it's worth,
for a trifle, a phrase, a gesture, a thought –
surely that's a reasonable premium?

Come on down then, come with your kind word…
Question is: how will you find one?

·1916·

A Moonlit Night

Landscape

The moon will rise.
It's already
a little bit risen.
There it is, hung all the way up above us.
It must be God,
using his wonderful
silver spoon
to scratch the stars' ears.

·1916·

To His Own Self, with Affection, the Author
Dedicates These Lines

A single verse.
Heavy as a punch in the mouth.
And he said unto them, Render therefore unto Caesar the things
which be Caesar's, and unto God the things which be God's.
But someone
like me –
where can I knock about?
Where have I built me an abode?

If I were
small as
the Pacific Ocean
I'd stand on the tiptoes of the waves,
at high tide pull myself close to the moon.
But where would you ever find me a lover
like myself? She wouldn't fit
in the itty-
bitty
sky!

Oh, if only I were a beggar!
Like a billionaire is!
What does money matter to the soul,
that insatiable plunderer?
The unchained horde of my desires
needs more than all the gold of California!

If only I could be inarticulate
as Dante
or Petrarch!
Fire up my soul for a single woman!
Order it in poems to burn down to ash!
My words
and my love

would form a triumphal arch:
and through it the greatest lovers of all time
would pass gloriously, and then vanish.

Oh, if only I were
silent
as thunder is,
I could make Earth's ruined shack quiver and tremble
with a single little moan.
If I roar
with the whole power of my enormous voice
then the comets wring their burning hands
and wretchedly cast themselves down.

I would gnaw at the night with my eyebeams –
oh, if only I were
dim like the sun is dim!
Yeah, like I'd really
want to
shine enough to calm
the Earth's skinny little bosom!

I proceed,
dragging my gigantic love.
On what night,
infirm
and delirious,
was I sired, by which Goliaths –
so enormous,
and so useless?

·1916·

To Russia

Here I come,
an ostrich from a distant land,
wearing these feathers: stanzas, metres, rhymes.
I foolishly try to bury my head,
dig it into my clinking plumes.

I am not yours, abominable snowland.
Soul,
burrow deeper into the down and fluff!
Mine is a different homeland,
I see
a sweltering southern life.

I'm amid palm trees on a baking island,
perfectly vased.
'Hey,
hit the road!'
They trample on my dreams.
So I go off again
to find a new oasis,
marking my tracks in the sands of time.

At first sight,
some people are unsure of me:
'Should I steer clear of it, does it bite?'
Others stoop to the lowest flattery.
'Mama, hey mama, does it lay eggs?'
'Beats me, dearest – it shouldn't, but might.'

The storeys whinny.
The streets stare.
I'm bathed in the water of frosts.
Riddled with smoke and pointing fingers,
I hurl yet another year into the past.
Alright, then, take me in your frozen grip!

Use the wind's razor to cut my feathers.
Exotic, outlandish,
I might as well vanish
under the fury of all Decembers.

·1917·

My Brother Writers

Obviously, I'm not going to get used
to the smart cafes and the smart people,
to drinking tea
and churning out line after line of lies –
I knock over the glasses,
climb onto a table.
My literary brothers,
lend me your ears!

You sit there
with your cups, dipping your little eyes.
The elbow's gone (all that writing!) in your velvet jacket.
Look up from your half-drunk glasses.
Brush your tangled hair back so you can hear better.

You,
oh, you bright young things,
clinging to the walls, thigmotaxic,
what got you
and the Word together?
You know,
François Villon robbed poor-boxes
when he wasn't putting pen to paper.

The beauty of this most magnificent age is entrusted
To you,
who even carry your penknives with care!
What's there to say about you?
There is a hundred times more interest
in the life of any lawyer's clerk.

Gentlemen,
have you really never got bored of palaces and courtiers,
dew-covered lilacs and the pang of love's dart?
If people like you are its creators
then I spit on any kind of art.

Better to float myself on the stock exchange,
or join some other, even shadier gang.
Stuff fat wallets into my gob.
Or, singing a drunken song,
cut out my soul in the back room of a pub.

All these long-haired writers, so overgrown,
that only one thought makes it through all this fuzz:
'Cut my hair? One haircut would be regarded a misfortune,
Two would look like carelessness.'

·1917·

The Revolution

A poetochronicle

26 February:
Drunken soldiers and policemen fired into the crowd.

27 February:
The light glowed red, and lingered.
Dawn spread and glinted on gun-barrels and blades.
In the dank barracks,
austere and sober,
the Volynsky Regiment prayed.

The company swore to the cruel soldier's god,
they beat their many-browed head against the ground.
Their blood was kindled, straining the veins in their heads.
Their hands angrily gripped the iron.

As for the first one, the man who had ordered:
'Shoot the starving people!'
A bullet closed his screaming mouth.
Someone started to speak: 'Squad…!'
He didn't finish.
He was stabbed.
The fury of the company burst out.

9 AM

In our usual place
in the Military Automobile School
we wait,
squeezed by the barracks fence.
Broken by doubts,
by the jitters of fear and joy we feel,
the dawn expands.

To the window!
I see,
from where the sky bites through
the lines of toothless alcazars,
up there the autocrat's eagle stretched and flew,
blacker,
crueller,
eaglier.

Suddenly –
people,
horses,
traffic lights,
houses,
and my barracks
in crowds
of hundreds
rushed out into the street.
The unbelievable noise! Our ears are attacked.
The road rings to the shattering sound of our feet.

And now from heaven knows where,
from the songs of the crowd,
from the bursting bronze of the guardsmen's
inhuman trumpets,
in a halo of broken dust, an image appeared.
She burns.
She reddens.

Wider and wider the wings extend.
Bread for the hungry,
water for those who thirst,
here she is:
'Take up your arms, citizens!
Citizens, take up your arms!'

On the wings of flags

like a hundred-headed lavaflow
she flew up from the throat of the city.
With the teeth of bayonets she bit into
the imperial eagle's black two-headed body.

Citizens!
Today the thousand years of the Past are over.
Today we revise the world's foundations.
Today we recut life to fit our cloth,
right down to the very last button.

Citizens!
This is the first day of the workers' flood.
The fleets head out hunting to the fury of sirens!
We go
To straighten out the tangled world!
Let the crowds hammer their noise into heaven!

Woe to the two-headed enemy!
And now it froths up, the singing.
The crowd's getting high.
The squares are bursting.
We rush forward in a tiny Ford,
outrunning the bullets that chase us persistently.
With the explosions of our car horns
we force our way into the city.

In the fog.
Steam rises from the river of the streets.
Like a dozen loaded barges in a gale,
there floats over the barricades,
creaking, the Marseillaise.

The first day's fiery cannon-ball
slid buzzing over the Duma's vault.
New day, new drivel,
a new shudder of new doubts.

What's going to happen?
Will they be thrown from windows,
or wait on plank beds in their cells?
Will the monarch once again
cover Russia with graves like molehills?

I muffle my soul against a sudden shot.
I hide it away under my overcoat.
The city rumbles, scattering the houses with machine-gun bursts.
The city burns.

Flames everywhere.
They rise and fall.
Scattering sparks, they rise higher.
These streets
taken by the red flag,
are a beacon calling out to Russia.

Again! O, again!
O, teach us more clearly, you red-tongued orator!
Squeeze the rays of the sun and the moon
with the vengeful fingers of thousand-armed Marat!

Death to the two-headed enemy!
Break down the doors to where the prisoners are,
their flesh torn with rusty talons.
With bundles of black eagle feathers
the policemen fall beaten.

The capital becomes a burning corpse.
Garrets were searched.
The time is near.
Crowds of troops
step onto the Troitsky Bridge.

A screech that shook the foundations.
We came together.

We fight.
Just one second later,
varnished by the setting sun,
the revolutionary flag hung like a flame from the Petropavlovsky
                                                                        fort.

Death to the two-headed enemy!
Strike off its heads with a single blow!
So it can never come to life again. Here it is! It falls away!
'Lord, gather these four thousand souls to your bosom.'
(Grasping at one last hope.)

Fair enough!
Every voice blares its joy up to heaven!
What need do we have
for any God? We've got saints enough of our own.

Why aren't you singing now?
Have you wrapped a Siberian shroud round your souls?
We've won!
Glory to us!
Gloooooory to us!

While the finger does not relax on the trigger,
a different will shall guide our way.
We will bring new tables of the law
down from our grey Mount Sinai.

To us, the villagers of the earth,
shall be given every village of the earth.
Brothers in our workshops, offices and mines.
We are the soldiers of the earth,
A life-giving battalion.

The motion of the planets, the existence of states:
all are subordinate to our wills.
The earth is ours.

The air is ours.
Ours are those diamond mines, the stars.
And we will never permit anyone to tear our earth with
                                        cannonballs,
to tear our air with the points of spears.

Whose wickedness broke the earth in half?
Who raised plumes of smoke over the butchery?
Is one sun for everyone not enough?
Is it not enough, the blue sky?

The last cannons join their bloody feud,
the last bayonets cut at the factories and mills.
We are made to scatter gunpowder.
We give children grenades as we used to give them balls.

These aren't the shouts of those who have nothing,
not cowardice crying from beneath a grey overcoat;
This is the thunderous roar of the population:
'I believe
in the greatness of the human heart!'

It rises above the dust of the battle,
above those who squabble, lose their faith:
on this day
an unheard-of occurrence poured forth:
the socialists' greatest heresy!

Petrograd

· 17 April 1917 ·

How Red is Your Riding Hood?

Once upon a time there lived a ConDem,[*]
red hat on his head, the most upright of men.

'Most upright of men', but aside from all that,
not a trace of red on him, apart from his hat.

The ConDem hears them say, 'The Revolution's startèd!'
Quick as a wink, the red hat's on his head.

They were merry as grigs: ConDem 1, ConDem 2,
the ConDem's old dad and his grandfather too.

But the weather then changed: the wind blew; the rain spat,
and one e-nor-mous gust tore to shreds the red hat.

And the ConDem was black. When they noticed this fact,
Revolution's red wolves got in on the act.

And everyone knows what a hungry wolf eats:
they munched that ConDem, from his nose to his cleats.

So when your political life starts, remember
the tale of the hat and the luckless ConDemmer.

·1917·

[*] Member or supporter of the Constitutional Democratic Party. The
explanatory note in the 1955 edition of Mayakovsky's *Complete Works* is a fair
summary of the Soviet attitude towards them: 'the Constitutional Democratic
Party of the liberal monarchist imperialist bourgeoisie in Russia. Covering
their true aims with liberal phrases, the CDs fought against the Revolution.'

Eat Your Pineapple

Eat your pineapple, chew your grouse:
your last day dawns, you bourgeois louse.

·1917·

Our March

Let the squares ring to the tramp of revolt!
Lift your heads' glorious mountain range higher!
We'll cleanse all the cities around the world
with a flood even greater than Noah's.

The days' bull's pied.
The years' cart creaks.
Our god is speed.
Our heart's drum beats.

Is our treasure, our gold, not the loftiest thing?
Can we ever be stung by the wasp of a bullet?
Our weapon's the songs that we sing.
Our voices are our gold bullion.

Lay yourself down, grass,
cushion the days' tread.
Rainbow, yoke the years'
galloping steeds' heads.

Look up! The skyful of stars is bored!
We weave our songs without the sky.
Hey, you there! Yes you, Great Bear!
Demand we be taken to heaven alive.

Drink up the joy! Sing!
The veins' spring's sprung.
Heart! Fight! Ring!
Our breasts are the copper of great kettledrums.

· 1917 ·

Spring

The snow is melted into drool.
The town's taken off its winter clothes.
Spring is here again, as foolish
and chatty as a sailor on shore leave.

· 1918 ·

How to Treat Horses

Hoofbeats.
Singing-like.
Clip.
Clot.
Clit.
Clack.

The street slipped:
shoes made of ice, drunk on the wind.
A horse crumpled
onto its crupper
and straight away, gawker
after bell-bottomed
gawker

came down Kuznetsky Street and crowded round,
laughter pealed and jangled.
'Hur hur, that horse done fallen!'
'Hur hur, fallen horse!'
Kuznetsky Street laughing.
Only I
didn't mix my voice with the general roars.
I went over
and saw the eye
of the horse.

The street had fallen over,
carried on as usual...
I went over and saw –
one vast teardrop after another slide
and roll down the muzzle,
hide in the horse's hide.

And some kind of generalised
beastly grief
plashed and poured out of me
and crept away crepitant.
'Hey horse, don't cry.
Hey horse, listen up:
why do you think they're better than you?'
Each of us
is a bit of a horse:
people are horses too.'
Maybe I was teaching her to suck eggs,
maybe my idea was so hackneyed its hair was grey,
but the horse jerked
and pulled herself up on her legs
then neighed
and walked away.
A chestnut child,
frisking her tail.
She came home happily

and stood in her box.
She felt like she was once again a foal,
that life was worthwhile,
that it was worth it to work.

·1918·

Ode to the Revolution

To you –
with the rude bayonets giving you ulcers –
to you –
catcalled,
butt of the whole regiment's jokes –
I joyously raise
over the soaring slander
my ode's triumphant
O!
O, brute!
O, infantile!
O, tuppenny-ha'penny!
O, magnificent!
What other names do they have for you?
What other plot twists do you hold, you little cheat?
Are you a Palladian palace
or a heap of ruins?
To the engine driver, covered in coal dust and ash,
or the miner digging down to seams of ore,
you burn incense, you burn reverential incense,
you glorify human labour.
But tomorrow –
hands up, don't shoot –
St Basil's Cathedral
will raise its cupolas uselessly,
and your piggish six-inch cannons will grunt

and blow up the Kremlin's thousand-year history.
And yeah, the good ship *Glory*
wheezes through her final trip.
Her sirens' scream drawn out and thin.
You send sailors
on board the sinking battleship
to where
there mewed a forgotten kitten.
And then!
You became a drunken crowd and roared.
Your devil-may-care moustache twirled with a swagger.
And it was grey-haired admirals you herded
with your gun-butts headfirst from the bridge in Helsingfors.
Your veins are exposed to the air again,
and you're licking and licking at yesterday's cuts.
So here you go: 'O, be cursed three times!' (this from the philistine);
and 'O, be four times blessed!' (this from me, the poet).

·1918·

Battle-Order to the Army of Art

They're still dragging out, the old duffer brigades,
their same drawn-out stories and tales.
Comrades, to the barricades!
The barricades of hearts and souls.
The only true communist's
the one who's blocked his escape routes.
That's enough walking, Futurists:
time for a leap into the future!
Building an engine's a tiny little thing –
screw some wheels on and Bob's your uncle!
But if there isn't a song to fill the station,
then what's the use of alternating current?
Load sound on top of sound

and then, forwards,
singing and whistling an air.
There are still some good letters around:
Ш,
Щ,
Р.*
It's not enough to form ranks – Eyes left! Eyes right! –
to earn more piping on your uniform.
A politician cannot make an army fight
if there are no musicians to play a march for them.
Drag pianos out onto the streets,
hang drums from the windows!
Beat them until they fall to pieces,
but make sure there's uproar,
and noise.
What's the point of toiling in factories,
getting dirt all over your face
and on your days off looking at others' luxuries
with sleep filling your blank eyes?
Enough of the same old rubbish.
Wipe clean your hearts.
The streets are our brushes.
The squares are our palettes.
In the thousand pages of time's manuscript
the days of revolution are as yet unsung.
Out into the streets, you Futurists,
poets and bangers of drums!

·1918·

*   Pronounced 'Sha, Shcha, Err.'

The Poet Worker

They shout at a poet:
'Why aren't you doing a real job, working a lathe, bolts and nuts?
Poems, so what?
I guess you just don't have the guts.'
Maybe
work
is more vital
to us than anything else.
I am a factory as well.
So what if I don't have chimneys?
I know:
you don't like flowery speech.
What a real man does is chop down the mighty oak.
But what are we
dealing with
if it isn't trees?
We use the oak of people's heads for our woodwork.
And yes,
it's a highly respectable thing to go fishing.
Haul in the net;
hope you catch a sturgeon!
But a poet's work's an even more respectable thing:
we're not fishers, but fishers of men.
It's a backbreaking task, to burn over a forge,
to temper the hissing iron.
But who could accuse us of slacking off?
We smooth brains with the file of our tongue.
Who's more important, the poet or the engineer
who brings people tangible benefits?
They are both as important as one another.
Souls are crafty engines; motors are hearts.
We are the same:
comrades in the working mass.
Body and soul: proletarians.
Only together can we beautify the universe

and tramp our feet to make the world ring.
We'll build a harbour for protection from the wordstorms.
Action stations!
Work is alive and new.
But people who talk rubbish: to the mills with them!
They'll turn the millstones with the rot they spew.

·1918·

Left March

As told to the Marines

Get together for the march!
No time for argument or rabble-rousers.
Barrack-room lawyers,
Shut it!
A few words
from comrade Mauser.
Enough of living by the laws
that date back to Eve and Adam's theft.
Let's flog history's dying horse.
Left!
Left!
Left!

Ahoy there, blue-jackets!
Over the oceans!
Full steam ahead!
The battleships used to have sharp keels:
have they been blunted?
Let the British lion mew,
baring his crown's spikes and clefts.
The commune never will be slaves.
Left!

Left!
Left!

There, past the mountains of sorrow,
is an unbroken sunlit land.
Past hunger,
past the plague-sea,
a million people stand!
Let armies of mercenaries surround us:
we can sense their steel's heft.
But the Entente will never crush Russia.
Left!
Left!
Left!

The agèd eagle winks an eye.
Shall we look back at all we've abandoned?
Seize the world by the throat
with your proletarian hands!
Draw yourselves up to your full height!
A red flag in every hand that's left!
Who's marching now with the right?
Left!
Left!
Left!

·1918·

Stunning Facts

No fact more unprecedented has ever been recorded
in the annals
of history:
through the hoarfrost, as the 'Internationale' sounded,
Smolny* rushed to the workers in Berlin yesterday.
And suddenly
all the eyewitnesses,
habitués of bars and the opera,
saw a three-storey
Russian spectre arise
and start to haunt Europe.
The café collapsed:
those who were eating their lunch
couldn't finish eating it,
and over Victory Lane a flag bunched:
'Power to the Soviets'.
In vain did people wring their pudgy hands –
that didn't stop its heedless career.
Smolny crushed them
and carried on over land,
crossing republics' and kingdoms' barriers.
And already from the lustre of the gleaming pavements
of Brussels, playing on people's nerves,
there arose the legend of the *Flying Dutchman*,
a *Flying Dutchman* of revolutionaries.
But Smolny went on across Flanders fields,
across the fields red with blood,
and rushed to shameful, treatyful Versailles.
He stood there, looming over Paris, red.
Smolny beckoned to the Parisians, playing a sweet march.
The Parisians stopped there, still.
He handed them a revolution, the Republic went smash

---

*   Smolny (the former Smolny Institute for the education of young noble-
women) was the site from which the early Soviet government operated.

and Smolny hopped over the Channel.
The cellars of London were poured out in its squares.
And then the steamships saw him pass,
low-slung, crossing the wide Atlantic over,
coming fast
to the Californian miners.
They say he turned human speech into gold.
These facts are dismissed by many biased observers.
But on Friday morning in America such a fire caught hold,
the earth itself seemed to be made out of gunpowder.
And if some whining Philistine were to say:
'Don't big up Russia, you're just kids bragging boastfully!',
I'd point him in the direction of what happened at Smolny,
to which I was a witness, yes, I, Mayakovsky.

·1919·

Vladimir Ilich!

I know:
a tale about a hero
is intelligentsia-style tripe!
There is no 'I' in Revoluton.
But who could hold back from a bit of hype
for Vladimir Ilich Lenin?

Legs without a brain are foolish.
Without a brain there's nothing for the hands to do.
A body without a head will rush
around like a chicken ditto.
We were being ruined, pummelled.
War howled loud enough to wake the dead.
When suddenly there rose over the world
Lenin's enormous head.
And the world settled back on its axis.

Every question had an answer that was simple and right.
And two creatures in the world's chaos
drew themselves up to their full height.
One was an animal, worse than an animal.
The other an unyielding mountain
who poured himself into billions of people.
The muscular mountain arose, maintained.

Now we know who our enemy is!
We do not miss the bullseye.
Our legs know which bodies
they are called upon to carry.

Some say: 'Wait!' Down with their snailish cries!
There is no space to doubt and whine.
Our hands know whom they should douse
with a deadly rain.

The earth is covered with fire and smoke:
wherever people seek their freedom,
the bomb of his name explodes:
Lenin!
Lenin!
Lenin!

This is not just a fan of poems unfurled
to hold over him like a wreath.
I believe in Lenin's world
and I also praise my faith.

And so I would not be myself
if I did not praise to the sky
and all its imagin'd corners
the Russian Communist Party.

·1920·

Vladimir Mayakovsky Rented a Dacha One Summer; You Won't Believe What Happened Next

Pushkino, on Akula Hill at the Rumyantsev Cottage,
twenty-seven versts along the Yaroslavl line.

Summer tumbled to its halfway point.
One sun? More like a hundred and forty!
It was hot,
a mazy heat:
this happened in the country.
The little Pushkino hillock arced
into Akula hill, and down the path
lay a tiny village, which smirked
with its crust of roofs.
And past the village was a hole
where the sun sank surely,
every evening without fail,
slowly and securely.
The next day he would rise again
to flood the world with light.
This happened day after day after day:
what a load of... rubbish!
And one day I got so annoyed
the whole world paled in fear,
and I shouted at him, point blank:
'Oy!
Stop rolling around up there!'
And then I shouted:
'Parasite!
In the clouds like some heavenly shogun!
While I don't know if it's day or night
as I sit here writing slogans!'
And then I shouted:
'Just a sec!
You, with your shiny physiognomy,
come on, you with your brass neck,

come inside and have some tea!'
I was for it now!
I'd gone and done it!
Towards me, of his own free will,
each footstep scattering rays of light,
the sun came up the hill.
Now, I don't want to show I'm scared
but I back away regardless:
he's getting close… he's almost here…
he's coming through the garden.
Through windows, doors, and cracks he pressed
and squeezed his sunny face;
once he'd squeezed in, he drew a breath
and spoke in a deep bass.
'I've forced the fires of heaven back
for the first time since creation.
You called me?
Right then, jam and cake!
And poet, put the kettle on!'
My eyes were filled with boiling tears,
the heat drove me insane,
but I showed him to the samovar,
said: 'Bright one, sit yourself down!'
The devil had made me impertinent,
and fired me up to shout and curse;
I sat embarrassed on the edge of a bench,
worried that things would get worse.
But he shone with some sort of clarity
and, forgetting to be formal,
I end up sitting comfy, chatty,
absolutely normal.
I talk about that,
I talk about this,
how work's driving me crazy (nearly),
and the sun says:
'Don't get your panties in a twist,
Just think about things clearly.

Do you think shining's just a piece
of cake? You should try it!
You move along – you've got no choice –
and shine with all your might!'
We talked and talked till night came on,
or at least until day would've ended.
What kind of darkness could there've been?
We chatted freely, friendly.
And soon, in open friendship now,
I slap him on the shoulder.
He slaps me back: 'Hey, me and you,
we're like a couple of brothers.
Come on poet, let's head out;
see the way the grey world's going.
I'll light it up with my sunny heat;
you light it up with your poems.'
The shadowy walls,
the imprisoning nights,
both fell to this double-barrelled sun.
A hotchpotch of poems and light:
shine with whatever you've got, shine on!
Say he gets tired, wants an early night,
the silly sleepyhead.
Then I shine out with all my might
and a new day leaps out of bed.
Shine everywhen,
shine everywhere,
until the last day dawns.
Keep shining on without a care:
that's my slogan, and the sun's!

·1920·

À la *Heine*

Her eyes shot me a lightning bolt:
'I saw you with her,
no point in hiding.
You're a cad, you're a wretch,
you're a dog, you're a dolt…'
On again,
on again,
chiding.
Look, dearest, I'm a big boy now,
all this ranting and grumbling… please, spare me.
If the lightning didn't strike me down,
then the thunder's
not going to scare me.

·1920·

Grief

The desperate wind vainly
beat unhumanly.
Drops of blood, blackening,
cover the roofs chillingly.
And out into the night
the widowed mood lonelied.

·1920·

A Story about How a Little Old Lady Spoke about Vrangel* without Understanding Anything

An old story of some practical use

Vrangel plods.
            We retreat.
Vrangel's allegedly winning.
Two little old ladies
               in the street,
queuing for food, and gossiping.
'My old man says,
              and he's not so dumb –
I believes him when he says so –
that that baron,
             yeah, you know the one,
is between Tver and Moscow.
And now they're selling
             for a song
all of Tver's
       rich
           plenty.
Forty pounds
        of flour...
            I'm not having you on...
one rouble twenty.
And as for vodka, just listen to this!
There's a cloud over Tver made of booze.
And everyone who goes out on the piss
gets taken home
           politely
             by the local fuzz.
Everyone, both left and right,

* Baron Piotr Nikolayevich Vrangel (1878–1928), leader of the White (anti-Bolshevik) forces in the Russian Civil War.

loves the baron's authority.
Maybe that's not the proper word, quite:
more like joy, simple equality.'

They stood there,
                    gabbing nineteen to the dozen.
Would he come, this figment?
Would he come,
                    this kingly baron
and his White contingent?

And then a wizard passed en route.
He said, 'Come on, old girl,
just slip on these seven-league boots,
we'll pop off to see your Vrangel.'
She put the boots on,
                         took a step,
and there she was in Tver.
Her husband had been talking crap,
the Soviets ruled there.
And then she tore around for days,
travelling at high speed,
to find the baron's flag in place
over Ai-Petri.
After viewing distant lands,
in an attempt to get things sorted
she settled down in a restaurant
that happened to be in Yalta.
In the Grand Hotel,
                      there Vrangel was,
chewing on some salmon.
Wider than the fish's jaws
the old lady's mouth swung open.
A maître d' saw her surprise
as she came in the venue:
he sidled over to her side
and handed her a menu.

The prices were mad, a kopek or two,
and a frenzy filled the old girl's heart.
'Right,' she said, 'bring me, right now,
the whole of the à la carte!'

The waiters raised dust as they came.
They broke into a sweat as
they brought her pork chops, well hung game,
fino sherry and *croquetas*.
She ate till her eyes popped, she ate her fill,
she ate so much she nearly burst!
Then finally
                    she called for the bill
in a trembling little voice.
They crowded round her, did some sums,
scribbled on scraps of paper,
agreed on a total – one hundred and one –
and handed the bill over to her.
'Now that's what I call reasonable!'
she thought as she looked at the docket.
She pulled two hundred roubles
out of her right-hand pocket.

The owner stepped back.
                    'No!' he said.
(His face was pale; sweat sprang to his pores.)
'Our roubles have been revaluèd,
they're worth a million times more than yours.'
The owner was furious, and started to yell:
'Don't you know the exchange rate?
There are no beggars in my hotel,
this is a place where the generals meet.'
The owner was furious, and started to shout:
'What the hell are you playing at, dearie?
Or do you think I'm here to give handouts
to every Tom, Dick and Harry?'
Now everyone angrily started to scream:

'We'll give you a meal to remember!'
And the owner, the guests and the maître d'
suddenly fell upon her.

When they heard the noise the local cop
immediately ran towards her.
The lady called to him:
                                'Make it stop!
Protect me, you force of order!'
But the force of order joined the fun
and eagerly put the boot in…
And a moment's work
                                saw him regain
all
      the old woman had eaten.

'Yes,' he said, 'life's great in Crimea,
if you're of the bourgeois persuasion;
but as for you,
                    it's time,
                                my dear,
to accompany me down to the station.'

But the woman
                    at the prison gates
jumped on a high-speed car
which took her back to her former place
in the RSFSR.*

Are they then representative citizens,
this pair of little old ladies?
Wouldn't you like to follow them
and visit that Crimean paradise?

·1920·

---

* The Russian Socialist Federative Soviet Republic, the official name for
Soviet Russia, at this time a sovereign state.

About the Filth

Glory, glory, glory to the heroes!

Alright,
change the record,
we've paid them tribute enough.
Now it's time to make some noise
about the filth.

The storm has died down in the Revolution's hearts.
The Revolution flaps like a fish in the slimy Soviet disarray.
And out from behind the
RSFSR
there creeps,
licking its whiskers,
the petty bourgeoisie.

(Hang on, don't take me literally here,
I'm not attacking the petty bourgeoisie outright.
It's the p. b. mindset that I've set out to 'flatter',
with no distinctions of class or estate.)

From every corner of Russia's boundless fields,
from the first day the Soviet system was established,
they flooded in,
changed their feathers quick as they could
and settled into every single office.

Five years' sitting and their bums are calloused,
they're as stolid as kitchen sinks,
living like they live, still waters running shallow,
who've flowed into comfortable studies and bedsits.

And in the evening, some scum or other
looks up at his wife – who's taking piano lessons – and says to her,
as he loafs by the samovar,

'Comrade Nadia, Comrade Nadia!
I got a raise,
My salary's twenty-four grand now.
Making my way up the scale.
Yeah,
I'll order some breeches, Pacific-Ocean blue.
I'll look like a breaching whale!'
And Nadya replies:
'Well, I'll need a whole new outfit;
everyone who's anyone's wearing hammer-and-sickle pattern twill.
What am I going to wear tomorrow night
at the Revolutionary Military Soviet Ball?'
They've got a portrait of Marx
in a crimson frame
and a kitten curled up on a pile of papers (revolutionary)
and from the ceiling hangs a gilded cage
where squeaks a frantic canary.

Marx stared at them fixedly from the wall…
then he opened his mouth to yell:

'Petty-bourgeois life is more terrible than Vrangel.
The Revolution's bound and gagged by these reactionaries.
They would do far better their songbirds to strangle,
if they don't want communism to be killed by canaries!'

·1920–1921·

All Meetinged Out

Every single day I see,
as soon as night gives way to dawn,
people heading to
Ltds,
Co.s,
PLCs
and to the committee room.
As soon as you go into any office
a thousand forms are your only greeting:
the employees have to make a careful choice
of fifty (!) of that day's (!) most important meetings.

You turn up and ask:
'Can anyone give me a moment?
I've been waiting here since the year dot.'
'Yes, but Comrade Ivan Vanich have got an appointment
with the Council for Rubbish and Rot.'*

You clamber up a hundred stairs.
The light is hardly flattering.
'Yes, but could you come back in a couple of hours?
It's the Working Group on Gossip and Nattering.'

A couple of hours
and the office is bare:
not a secretary, sub-secretary, sub-sub-secret'ree!
Everyone younger than twenty-two years
is out at the Young Communist League.

Up the stairs once again, as the twilight grows thicker,
to the office's penthouse suite.

---

* The combination of singular subject and plural verb in this sentence is
deliberate in the Russian.

'Ivan Vanich?' 'Yes, but…' An undisguised snicker:
'He's with the board of Immakingthisup PLC.'

Furious,
I burst into the meeting like lava,
belching out curses to anyone in my path.
And I see
(it looks like an odd kind of slaughter)
that the room is filled with people cut in half.
'They've killed them!
They've chopped them!'
I run around, barmy.
The terrible sight's forced me out of my mind.
Then I hear the secretary's torso
speak very calmly:
'We're in several meetings at the same time.
Every day we've got to do around twenty,
so although it's inconvenient we all are for the chop.
Down from the waist went to room 7B,
and the ones who stayed here are the tops of the top.'

I'm so stressed I can't sleep.
The small hours are coming.
A thought comes to my mind as an early dawn greeting.
'We should get everyone together, send out a summons:
hold one more meeting on abolishing meetings!'

·1922·

Bastards!

I've hammered my lines into you, nail by nail,
now shut the fuck up.
Listen to my wolfish howl
that barely pretends to be a poem.
The fattest of you,
the baldest,
come over here and see!
Grab them by the collar!
Let's look at the report from the Famine Committee.
There,
behind the naked columns of figures…

The wind lunged around.
Quietly lunged…
And again the snow heaped together
the Volga villages
into their thousand-million-roofed grave.
The chimneys are grave-candles.
Even the ravens
vanish,
sensing that,
with the chimneys' heat,
there rises
the sickly,
nauseating
smell
of frying greasy meat.
A mother?
A daughter?
A father?
A son?
Who is it?
Who's next in the cannibal line?

There will be no help!
The air is empty.
There will be no help!
They are cut off by the snows.
There will be no help!
Beneath their feet
The very earth's been gnawed at
and no grass grows.

No,
no help!
They have to give in.
Count the graves in this part of the country!
Twenty
million!
Twenty!
Million!
Lie down
and die!

It is only the earth alone that cries,
in a husky voice,
its mad curses blown white by the storm-filled skies,
the wind raking its snowy hair of roads and rivers.

Bread!
A crust!
A crumb!

Seeing death face to face,
barely eating,
almost dead:
it's its working hand the city stretches
for a handful of dry bread.

'Bread!
A crust!

A crumb!'
The radio calls out over every border,
And answers are given,
dumb and ever more dumb,
in the pages of the papers.

'London.
A banquet.
Attended by kings and queens.
As a gesture, the guests' seats will not be golden.'

Damn you! God damn you all to hell!
I hope savages come from the colonies you conquered,
hungry and cannibal,
hunting your head
with its crown!
I hope your cities are burnt to the ground!
I hope the flame of rebellion burns
brightly over your kingdom!
I hope that – in copper cauldrons! –
your sons and heirs are boiled into jam!

'Paris. A parliamentary gathering.
A report on the famine.
Fridtjof Nansen.
He listened with a smile, as if it were a nightingale's song,
or a tenor singing a fashionable romance.'

Damn you! God damn you all to hell!
I hope for centuries you hear no human voice!
French proletariat!
Instead of a speech for these thick necks, implacable,
why not try weaving a noose?

'Washington.
Farmers, having first of all
eaten

and drunk their fill,
their bellies filled with swan meat,
scuttle into the ocean –
they're drowning in excess wheat –
ships with their cargoes of corn.'

Damn you! God damn you all to hell!
I hope that – in the spot where it hurts the most –
your streets are filled with rebels
North and the South, East and West Coast,
and that they drive your belly-footballs
from pillar to post!

'Berlin.
The émigrés are joyous.
Whole groups of them are joyful:
they'd be happy, if they had the choice,
to fight these starving people.
Twirling his moustaches,
moving at a trot,
boastfully through Berlin there passes
the true Russian patriot!'

Damn you! God damn you all to hell!
An eternal 'fuck off' to all of you pests!
To every single twisting Judas smile
chasing French gold: may you never find rest!
Russian forests,
gather together!
Pick out your biggest aspen.
Set it so they can always see it silhouetted there,
and remember what they're missing.

'Moscow.
The complaints from those who shake collecting tins:
"In all the fancy restaurants I've been
they either wince
or give you a three-rouble bit, worth nothing since 1918."'

Damn you! God damn you all to hell!
I hope you burn your throat on every mouthful
each time you swallow!
Or the knife bounces back
from your juicy steak
and cuts your belly open!

They are dying.
Twenty million people are dying!
And they are damned as of now,
they are damned forever:
the names of everyone who keeps silent
and turns his fat face away from the Volga.
These words are not for the comfy and fat
or those who wear the royal coronet:
words will never stick them in the heart
(for that you need the Revolution's bayonet).

But they are for you,
the army of individual atoms,
the world's strong gunpowder,
whose force, when thrown into every basement,
will blow up the rich in vast numbers!
For you! For you! For you!
You are my words' target.
With these figures, scarcely able to be contained,
set down like waymarks,
the Volga calls the bourgeoisie to account.

The fire will come!
Burnt offering and catharsis.
The palaces of the pitiless rich will burn
and the fire will prove equally pitiless
on the day of retribution.

·1922·

The Bureaucratiad

Bureaucracy's great-grandmother

A street.
A vending machine.
You stick in your five kopek bit.
Hissing nastily, something gives a turn.
Two minutes later, a three-kopek chocolate slides out.
Why do you crowd around rubbernecking,
sheeple?
In a shop it'd be easier and better,
and cheaper.

Yesterday's version

The devil, his son,
or their brother
puffed these chocolate machines up into offices
and posted them all over the RSFSR,
ignoring all checks and balances.
By night shadows had turned into people.
And the office door squeals
like a drawbridge being raised, and swallows
a wriggling human tail.

The door was half closed:
still the entrance was insufficiently narrow.
Through the office barricade's bars,
grabbing their pass, walk the chosen few.
A human river poured down the corridors.

(The first cruel wound –
the first injured howls –
'That guy jumped the queue!'
'He should get sent down!')

Seek, and ye shall find:
go and stir them up!
Which queue's going down,
and which one's coming up?
And after an hour or two, you finally see someone.
'A rouble for the paper? That's a joke!'
And they poke a trembling hand
between the jaws of the entry-book.
The wheels started to turn.
From under-secretary to under-secretary
a piece of paper ran,
its annotations a thing of beauty.

And then the paper made it to the real func-
tionaries. Six of them, from the junior to the head!
By the time it reached the sixth: lunch.
She went out to lunch and the trail went dead.
Don't try to count the stars:
it'll drive you insane.
Don't try to work out who's in charge:
it'll do the same.
The paper floated at a sluggish pace.
The machine turned lazily round its axles.
The paper was stuffed into pockets and poked into briefcases
and filed on shelves and placed on tables.
Under a heap of similar friends
the paper waited to be picked up
and throughout its many-months-long isolation,
it dreamt of its 33% markup.

Its papery body grew fatter at first.
Then bulldog-clip feet came and clamped it together.
Then it stopped being paper and became a 'case'
and moved into a large dark blue folder.
The director gloriously wrote all over it,
then it went to his deputy, back down the chain:
the deputy signed, and with a cover note

it went to be signed by the director again.
We thought there was no unsigned space left,
but once again
the machine
took hold of the paper,
and sprinkled stamps and seals like dandruff
on every
as-yet-untouched
gap.
And look,
after only a year,
the exit-book opened its mouth with a scraping of quills
and threw out a piece of paper –
a revalued, worthless draft for a million roubles.

Today's version

Their mouths open wide, their tongues hanging out,
the NEPmen* are driven by zeal and fury...
And among them
rear up
the unbreachable forts,
the grey castles of the Soviet bureaucracy.
Dressed in their paper armour,
rattling their spiny quills,
the workers carried on until at the door
a paper appeared:
'cutbacks in personnel!'
Without any upset, without any panic,
the wheels of the office started to click.

---

* The NEP, or New Economic Policy, is the name given to a series of economic reforms inaugurated in Soviet Russia after the Civil War in order to boost the economy. It allowed small-scale capitalist enterprise and, not surprisingly, led to the creation of a class of individual, the NEPman, who profited from the relaxation of the rules. This is one of a number of poems in which Mayakovsky speaks out against these people whom he viewed as profiteers.

Number one picked it up.
Number two put it back.
The paper went forward.
The paper went back.
Along the path blazed by other
pieces of paper
it went to the deputy
and then on to safety.
And the next week the board debated the facts:
'How many more clerks do we need to contract?'

Everyone on the board argued staunchly.
They decided to work at top speed,
and immediately elected a steering committee,
which elected a new board and sub-board.
The committee was working flat out,
was working so hard that it started to sweat.
They drew up a plan
made of circles and lines,
the most glorious reds, most veridical greens.
A hundred extra workers, all supernumerary,
who worked at the weekend and through every holiday.
Sitting at their stations,
bent over heaps of paper,
they flaunt their calculations,
burrow deeply into numbers.
Their throats parched,
mouths foaming,
the question was brought to the plenary once again.
Everyone made proposals, soberly and wisely:
'Sack half the workforce!'
'A major downsizing!'
The secretary took minutes,
all in a sweat:
they enacted a decree,
a decree was enacted...
All night long,

bent low over her smoking machine
the typist tapped out resolution after resolution.
And…
the place was deserted,
not a worker survived,
and little stray cats
built their dens in the archives.

My resolution

I think that you'll find –
if you pause to take stock –
that this is a story about a BULL and a COCK.

A concrete suggestion

I,
as you know,
am no manager or secretary.
I'm a poet with absolutely no bureaucratic capacity.
But I think
that it's necessary –
would be a mercy –
to take
the offices by the chimneys and give them a good shake.
And then to sit down
with the workers you'd shaken out,
and pick up just one of them,
and say to him:
'Write!'
With just one proviso,
a finishing touch:
'You go ahead, comrade, and write, *but not much*!'

· 1922 ·

I Love

Normally, it's like this

For every living creature there's an allowance of love made,
but what with work
and earning a living,
etcetera,
the heart's soil where that love might be cultivated
grows every day harder and drier.
Apparently, it's not enough
that the heart wears a body,
and the body, a shirt.
Some man –
an idiot –
invented cuffs
and covered his breast with starch.
Old age focuses the mind.
Makeup gets smeared on women.
Men mill their arms, commanded by Müller.*
But it's too late.
Wrinkles colonise the skin.
Love blooms,
and blooms,
and then boringly withers.

When I was a child

I was given the love that was owed me.
But from childhood
people
are drilled in their duties.
Not me,
I ran off to the river Rioni

---

* Jørgen Peter Müller (1866–1938), author of popular gymnastics text-
books, in particular *My System* (1904).

and loafed by its banks,
playing hooky.
My mother got angry:
'You lousy little brat!'
My father threatened to give me a hiding to remember.
But I,
rich to the tune of a false three-rouble note,
played three-card Monte down by the fence with the soldiers.
No shirts to weigh me down,
no shoes to burden me,
I'd bake in the Kutaisi heat.
I'd offer the sun first my back,
then my belly,
until my gut told me it was time to eat.
The sun was surprised:
'You can hardly see him, he's so small!
But he's got a heart,
you can see how it strives.
How can he
be bounded
in that nutshell,
and find room for me,
and the river,
and the cliffs?'

As a youth

There's lots of things to do for a young 'un.
We teach grammar more foolishly than any fool.
They kicked me out of class
when I was ten.
Sent me to Moscow prisons for my school.
In your tiny
apartment world,
curly lyrics grow, only fit for the boudoir.
What substance is there to these poetic lapdogs?
I was taught
about love

in Butyrka.*
I don't care that you're sighing for the Bois de Boulogne!
Or that you're mooning around because you saw the sea!
I fell in love with the 'Bureau of Funeral Preparations'
through the peephole in cell 103.
Others look at the sun every day,
overweening:
'How much, do you reckon, could we charge for that light?'
For the little yellow hare
that passed over the ceiling,
I would have given the world, would have given my life.

My university

You can speak French.
Multiply.
And divide.
You know your declensions.
Go ahead, then: decline!
But tell me:
can you and a building
sing a duet?
Do you understand the language of the tramline?
A human chick,
newly out of its shell,
reaches for books,
starts to note things down.
But I used shop signs to learn the alphabet,
leafing through pages of iron and tin.
Others take up the earth,
slice it and scrape it,
and that's how they learn, a tiny globe in the round.
But it was with my ribs that I studied,
as I lay down

---

* Prison in central Moscow in which Mayakovsky was imprisoned in 1909, charged with revolutionary activities.

to spend the night
on the ground!
Questions to keep a pop historian turning in his bed:
'Was Barbarossa's beard really red?'
Let them worry!
I won't root through similar rot –
but I know every story that Moscow's got!
They take up Dobroliubov,* to generate hatred
of evil, but his name means 'lover of good'.
His family tree stands against it
their complaints grown deep into the wood.
From an early age I've
learnt to hate the fat,
as I had to sell myself
to get fed.
Others stuff themselves with study,
then stay sitting around –
if they ever want to woo a lady,
little thoughts clank from their tiny brass brows.
But I grew up speaking
to buildings.
My only interlocutors
were water-towers.
The rooftops would catch every word I let go,
carefully listening with every window.
And then they'd gossip
about the night
or their friends,
their weathervane tongues twisting in the wind.

When I became a man

Grown-ups are busy.
Pocketfuls of roubles.

---

* Nikolai Aleksandrovich Dobroliubov (1836–1861), literary critic and revolutionary.

You want love?
Of course!
It'll cost you a monkey.
But I,
homeless,
stuck my huge hands in the holes
where my pockets had been,
and walked around, gawking.
It's night.
You get dressed up: looking good!
You go off to relax with some widows or wives.
But it was in the embrace of her endless ringroad
that Moscow held me and stifled.
In your hearts,
those little clocks,
your lovers are ticking, metred and rationed.
Your partners in the love bed are in raptures.
But, lying out on the square of Our Lady of The Passion,
it was the wild heartbeats of the city I captured.
Turned inside out,
my heart almost on my sleeve,
I open myself to the sun and the wet.
Come here with your passions!
Climb aboard with your love!
From now on I'm not in control of my heart.
With other people, I know where their hearts must be.
Stuck in their chests – any child knows that!
But in my case –
a whole different crazy anatomy –
my heart's omnipresent, I'm nothing but heart.
How many seasons there are,
only counting the springtimes,
heaved into my ardent heart over the last twenty years!
Literally –
I mean literally, not like in a poem –
their unreleased weight is too much for me to bear.

What happened

Bigger than it could possibly be,
far bigger than it needed to be,
a poetical frenzy rearing up in a dreamstate –
this lump that was my heart spreading out, growing bulky:
a lump made of love,
a lump made of hate.
Under this burden
my legs shook
and shuddered
(although
you know
I'm a pretty strapping fellow):
I'm still dragging this heart-shaped appendage
bent like a ploughman following his furrow.
I swell with the milk of poems
and cannot drain my breasts:
there isn't any point – they just fill up again.
Lyrics exhaust me –
I'm the world's wet-nurse
(just to turn to hyperbole
the original image from Maupassant).*

I call out

I hoisted my heart like the Pocket Hercules,
spun it around like an acrobat.
Like they call in the voters, or raise the alarm when a fire blazes,
I called out:
      'Here it is!
      Here!
      Take it!'
When such a lump sighed and huffed,

---

* Reference to Guy de Maupassant's short story 'Idylle' (1884), in which a
young man on a train helps relieve a woman who is travelling to start a job as
a wet-nurse by suckling her milk-swollen breasts.

every lady at once
shot away like an arrow,
through the dust,
through the dirt,
through the snowdrifts:
'We'd like something smaller,
gentler, like a tango...'
I cannot carry my burden
and yet I carry it.
I want to throw it away,
yet I will not throw it away.
I bear it, not peacefully like some caryatid,
but with my whole body cracking under the strain.

You

You came along
businesslike,
looked past
my size
and my roars,
and saw nothing more than a little boy.
You picked up
my heart
like a girl
picks up a ball,
and went away to play.
And all the other women
considered it some kind of miracle:
every girl
and every woman stood there edgily.
'Love someone like that?
Ones like that never settle.
She must be a lion tamer.
She must be from the menagerie!'
But I rejoice.
The yoke is lost!

Forgetting myself in this joy,
I leapt
and jumped like an Indian wedding guest
I was so happy
and easy.

Impossible

I can't do it alone,
I can't lift a piano
(even less
a fireproof safe).
And if a safe
or a piano's
a no-no,
then how
could I carry my heart
if I took back my love?
Bankers are savvy:
'We're rich beyond measure.
No room in our pockets –
to the safe with our treasure!'
To store my love
with you
is like safely caching gold pieces.
I hid it and now
I can stroll
as rich as Croesus.
And perhaps
if I really want to,
I'll take out a smile,
a smile-ha'penny,
a smile-farthing,
and if I'm out with my friends on a spree,
I'll spend all my lyrical small change by morning.

And also with me

The navy comes home and flocks to the port.
Trains hurry home to their terminal.
The force that makes me hurry towards
you – I'm in love! – is more powerful.
The covetous knight in Pushkin's play
goes down to the cellar to tally and calculate.
And I always come back to you in that way
my darling, to admire my own heart.
You scrape off the dirt, shave and wash,
you always come joyfully back to your home.
And that's how I come home to you,
for when I come to see you, I am coming home.
The earth's womb takes in all earthly things.
At the end we return to our goal.
And so I reach out
to you
unswerving,
hardly have I departed:
I barely leave at all.

Conclusion

Love won't be bleached away
by arguments
or miles.
It's been considered
and tested,
and proved.
I solemnly swear, lifting my poem's finger-lines:
unchangingly and faithfully,
I love!

·1922·

Worker Correspondent

For five years the workers' throats have sung;
our love will praise the workers for a century –
will tell how
                        in battle
                                    they showed themselves
                                                            strong
against Entente powers
                            armed to the teeth.
The bourgeoisie went wild.
                                    The whole universe
existed to serve them.
                            Theirs were the tanks
with hides impossible to pierce.
Theirs were the billions
                            in roubles
                                        and francs.
And finally,
                with pencils,
                                a forest of pens,
thousands of bourgeois hacks
bristling up
                in their class's
                                    defence,
poured balm on the bourgeoisie,
                                        tar on the workers.
We lashed our steeds,
                            we beat our foreheads,
swam through bloody rivers,
                                    crawled across bloody sands.
We took
            Perekop,
                        the most fortified fortress,
practically with our bare hands.
By our strength
                    we calmed

their strength

that came furious.

The beastly herd's

banished

and beaten.

But there's a whole fortress remains –

their ideas,

their bayonet-pens bristling.

It is time to forge the final weapon.

Take up the pen in our hands.

It is time

to fight back

with the pen.

It is time

to use the pen

to defend.

Scrawling all over innumerable scraps,

struggling to unspool their thoughts' ribbon,

by night the worker-correspondents scratch away,

and the peasant-correspondents.

We write,

absorbing the workers' sorrow,

will we be painted over by some trifler's varnish?

We know:

millions of future truths will grow

from our present-day sketches.

If he got his revenge,

the enemy would be glad.

The bureaucrats' attitude is fissile.

The workers

are doused

by the Sovbureaucrats

with denunciations and dismissals.

We will strike truly.

It is time to strike.

The kulak

trembles

under the pen.

A hero takes up a pen to fight flies.
Against the hero
                    knives are sharpened.
But no!
          The knife will not be held against any throat.
And again
              we will bend our arm over the page.
The kulak's imprisoned
                          by the people's court.
And the director of *Pravda* is purged.

Protecting all our working friends,
shoving away the enemy swarm,
long live
          the red
                    worker's pen
our present-day weapon!

·1923·

A Universal Answer

I'm tired
          of writing notes:
writing anything hurts.
I suggest,
              with no unnecessary words,
a universal answer
                    to everyone at once.
If some soldier
                or other
wants us
          to promote a war,
our reply would go:
no!

And if,
           even with the most intractable problems
someone stretches out a hand
                              and asks for a conference,
then we would acquiesce:
yes!
And if some dictator
tries to scare us with an ultimatum,
our reply would go:
no!
And if,
           avoiding the ultimatum situation,
they say 'let's talk about reparations',
then we would acquiesce:
yes!
If
   the concessions
                    included a clause
that would lead us
                    to crush the necks of the workers,
our reply would go:
no!
And if,
           mutually
                    unlacing a tightly closed purse,
                                        they suggest,
'let's work together,
                    let's all be honest!'
then we would acquiesce:
yes!
And if they want
                    to stick their
                                   snout in
on the question
           of who's condemned
                              and who is pardoned,
our reply would go:

no!
And if they simply
                want to
                        ask a favour
(forgive me the expression)
                        these poor old fools
then we would acquiesce:
yes!
Curzon,
        Poincaré,*
                and who else?
Please don't
        ignore this note:
before firing off angry epistles,
read the poem
                what I wrote.

·1923·

---

* George Curzon (1859–1925), British Secretary of State for Foreign
Affairs; Raymond Poincaré (1860–1934), the French prime minister.

Baku

Baku.
A town of wind.
The sand spits in your eye.
Baku.
A town of fires.
Blazing Balakhan.*
Baku.
Leaves are flakes of ash.
Branches are cables.
Baku.
The streams are oil-ink.
Baku.
Flat-topped buildings.
Hunchbacked people.
Baku.
No one moves there for fun.
Baku.
Grease stain on the world's jacket.
Baku.
A reservoir of dirt,
but I am drawn to you
                    by a love
                            that is greater
than that which attracts
                        dervishes to Tibet,
Christians to Jerusalem,
                        the faithful to Mecca.
In Baku
        are machines that sigh
with billions of
                wheels and pistons.

---

* Area near Baku containing some of the country's oil refineries.

They kiss,
                then they kiss again
                                tirelessly,
quietly bringing up oil
                        by suction.
In a chain
            of paralysed bodies,
not daring
            to oppose
                    the city's desires,
there crawls to Baku,
                    obedient,
a writhing snake of tankers.
If the future's
            a place
                    you can fully believe in
it is because
                the capitals' hearts
                                are filled
up to the brim
with thick,
            black,
                    Baku blood.

·1923·

Moscow-Königsberg

Out on the highways, fewer people to meet.
Canny Moscow
        is snoring still.
Eating up Tver Street,
           tearing up Tver Street
comes the forty horse-power Cadillac.
Its radiator
      brushed away
           the horizon
              like a fan.
Eins!
   Zwei!
    Drei!
        The noise of the motor.
A door into the sky –
        the aerodrome.
Brik.
   The mechanic.
        Newbold.[*]
           The pilot.
Things.
    Five kilos of luggage each.
          Five people on board.
The earth lurched.
      The roads ran away
          like lizards.
Like a tablecloth
      Khodynka[†] spread.
The red army barracks
       on Khodynka
          slid backwards.
 Sky,

[*] D. I. Newbold, English Communist.
[†] Khodynka, an area of Moscow near the Petrovsky Park.

is that you,
                    and are those the stars?
Past the stars
                    (don't forget your visa)!
Through the sky,
                    past everything we pass,
it all falls away,
                    the earth flying away beneath us.
Something like the sun
                    above us,
                              turning.
And time
          went off
                    to behave abnormally.
The towns
          through the cracks in the clouds
                              are shining.
A bird tries to catch us,
                    doesn't make it,
                              falls away…
Pits in the air.
          We whoop
                    at the tops of our lungs.
Lightning flashed alongside us.
                              Newbold frowned.
In our ears and around them,
                    the motor's thrum.
But no annoyance,
                    no pain.
Heart, beat faster!
Catch the motor's rhythm.
I
  and the motor
sweetly merged together.
'From a cliff
Icarus and his wings were thrown
so that this airy river

to Königsberg might flow.
All those sketches and designs
exhausted Leonardo
so that I might fly
wherever I needed.
They crashed and burned,
all those great aviators,
and now, clipping the sun,
I traverse Lithuania.
Roland Garros
beat every record
so I could cross
these mountains of clouds.
Hugo Junkers
with his engines did tinker,
so the noise of the motor
might rival the thunder.'
So, what?
       You say Icarus
              had to expire,
and men had to wilt,
          at work in the factory,
so that some guy –
          Vladimir Mayakovsky,
               esquire –
could swoop into Königsberg
           for a holiday?
So that a wingless and tailless bird
could settle his bum on the pillows of clouds?
So I could peel a sausage
         and carelessly throw
the trash
     on the valleys
        and cities below?
No!
    Squeeze your shoulders
         out of this flying pulpit
Look one hundred faces

straight in the face!
And you,
          tomorrow's,
                    day-after-tomorrow's
                              people,
My invincible,
          iron-fisted
                    class,
thank you,
          a chain has been forged
                              on this flight
between you and me,
                    the weakest link.
I look out over you,
                    land of work and sweat,
at the flaming wreath
                    of the horizon.
We have taken to the air,
                              but not that much as yet.
If it turns out
          we need
                    to build a stairway to Mars,
please,
          be kind enough
                    to let me give my life for it.
Do you want me to jump down
                              from three thousand metres?

· 6 September 1923 ·

Mad about the Movies

Europe.
  A city.
     Eyes ransacked by all there is to see.
Multicoloured drops
     into the eyes
       dropped in.
On every lamppost
    for miles
      any-old-how,
        CHARLIE
CHAPLIN!
A crumpled little man
    from Los Angeles
crosses
  the ocean
    with his pair of roller skates.
And anyone
   who has eyes to see
laughs till they're helpless,
      laughs till their belly aches.
A well-heeled dandy (in pickled winkle-pickers) –
screw him!
   The matron figure (her chest is stacked).
Lunch.
  A chicken.
    Right in the face –
      the same chicken.
A motorbike.
   A crowd.
    A detective.
     A shriek.
A kick up the bum.
   A blow to the face.
A black eye.
  A thick ear.

Jelly-chins wobble playfully.
The theatre's filled with a million
                              laughing profiteers.
Shut up,
        Europe,
                you transparent fool!
Muses,
        your springs
                no longer flow.
I don't believe in you,
                I don't know you,
above every one of you,
                laughing,
                        stands Charlot.
Pin-headed.
                Fat-bellied.
Europeans,
            why do you need to increase?
Isn't
    the Chaplin moustache
                        the only element
That remains
            of Europe's face?
Charlot.
        His bunchy trousers sag.
His quiff.
        His battered bowler hat.
Making
        a mockery
                of your mosquito legs,
O Europe
        of the high tea
                and the dinner jacket.
The theatre
        is filled
                with a chattering crew

of girls,

      as Charlie chauffeurs some sneering pup.

Will you please be quiet, please!

             The joke's on you.

Europe,

     clear your throat,

          sit down,

              shut up.

Chaplin,

    go on,

        throw that custard pie.

Well,

   it needn't be a pie,

        needn't be on film.

They will arise,

      the forgotten people,

          and they

will sweep

     the world clean

         with a slapstick broom.

In the meantime,

      Russia,

        keep cranking the camera.

A fight! We came here to see this!

A worldwide sensation.

        One last touch of drama.

An angel-winged Chaplin.

       Charlot's apotheosis.

·1923·

Be Prepared

A fool said to another fool: 'Sure!
There'll be no trouble from the Ruhr.
German actions are no basis
to get our knickers in a twist.
And England's too far across the sea
to cause trouble
                    for you or me.
We need to deal with Afghanistan?
I don't think it needs
                    to be part of the plan.'
This is what a dimwit said.
If you're clever,
                    you look ahead.
If Mr Hughes* is crawling about,
the boot is on the other foot.
And if Curzon enters the dispute,
the boot's on the other other foot.
And it'll be on the third foot
                    (if there is one)
whenever news comes through from Poland.
We'd gladly
              lay
                    our rifles down
but we'll still keep looking round
in case our enemy's providing cover
for some new Vrangel
                    or another.
The French,
         the bourgeois,
                    all our enemies
have heavy fists
              and bottomless bellies.

---

* Charles Evans Hughes (1862–1948), at that time US Secretary of State.

We can't feed the German hosts:
they will soon be at our throats.
Should we laze around our homes?
No,
    we must purge ourselves from dreams.
We need to know
        what's going down
and take it all into account.
Read the military news
and carefully establish views.
Tell the world, spread the word:
be on guard
    and be prepared!

· 1924 ·

Kiev

The boughs of the pine trees,
        small ones
          large ones…
All covered in snow,
    but still so cosy!
As if
    I were visiting
        an old,
          old woman,
I arrived in Kiev yesterday.
And now
    I stand
        on the hill of Saint Vladimir,
the vista too wide
    for your arms to embrace!

This was how,
   way back when,
      in the frost shining clear,
Perun the thundergod
     looked down on Kievan Rus.[*]
And then,
   though who it was
      and when
        I don't rightly remember,
I only recall that it was down there
on the ice,
   by the water,
      through the rapids,
        by portage,
that they
   brought tribute
      to Askold and Dir.[†]
And then
   the sun
     beat the cupolas like timpani.
'Bow down and stay still.
      Rus, fall to your knees!'
Even today
   Vladimir
      urges us to the monasteries.
The stone saint holds tight
      to the whip of the cross.
And from these places,
     beyond the back of beyond's back,
came our great,
   great-great,
      and great-great-great-grandfathers!

---

[*] During the period of pagan reaction (tenth century) preceding the conversion of Kievan Rus to Christianity, the hill near the royal palace above Kiev displayed an important idol of Perun, god of thunder in Slavic mythology.
[†] According to the chronicles, Askold and Dir were rulers of Kiev in the late ninth century.

My grandmother has many such
                              bloodline knick-knacks,
here on the banks of the Dnieper.
They killed Stolypin,*
                    then brought him back as a sculpture,
a monument,
                two fingers stuck up
                                  into his uniform.
He was killed again,
                      the lime-trees swayed
                                    in the crossfire
as control of the government
                          rattled back and forth.
Kiev's bosom hums
                as the heat from the boilers rises
just as
      the smoke
              rises from the factories.
It's not a heavenly
                  but an earthly Vladimir who baptises us
with the iron
            and fire
                  of decrees.
The view's even making me
                        forget
                              I'm a Russophile.
Well,
    I'm still a Russophile,
                        but cut from a different cloth.
Here is my working country,
                        alone in the
                                  whole wide world.
'Hey,
      Poincaré,

* Piotr Arkadievich Stolypin (1862–1911), Imperial Russian Prime
Minister, assassinated in a Kiev theatre.

want to look after us?'
                              Fuck off!
So,
    let one last
                ancient
                        old man
                              make the bells weep
in the monastery bell-tower.
                              Let the wolfish shout
rise
    one more time
                    from Kiev's main street:
'Currency bought and sold here!
                              Favourable rates!'
Our strength is the truth,
                          your strength is your tinkling symbols.
Ours is the smoke from factories,
                              your smoke comes from
                                        burning myrrh.
You keep your currency exchange,
                              we have the hearts of the people.
We will take it all,
                we will capture
                          and conquer.
Ave atque vale,
                grey-haired old lady!
Get out of the way!
                Hurry up!
                          Get a move on!
Lay down and die,
                speculator,
                          wide-boy!
We march on –
                the band of your youthful grandchildren!

·1924·

Two Berlins

Sliding
        along
                the Ku'damm in my car,
astonished,
                I blink my eyes:
compared
        to how it was
                        if you go back a year,
Germany
        is a completely different place.
On first sight,
a general impression:
the Germans are fed;
the Germans don't complain.
The dollar
            used to be
                        their single bright spark,
and now it's
            '*Entschuldigung!*
                        We only take marks.'
The German
            parades
                        through the city proudly,
where before,
            like water,
                        he used to fearfully stumble,
because of that one thing,
                        a hard currency,
even one's smile
            becomes
                        hard as marble.
Doubtfully
        I look at
                each satisfied face:

why then
          is the city
                    so full of police?
I wander
          and sniff at
                    the workers' district, Nord.
Want,
          skinnily,
                    bursts upon the eyes.
You hear conversations:
                    'Yes, the Wolffs died...
from hunger...
          the family...
                    turned on the gas...'
I get it –
          a stupid child would get it –
you just need to come here
                    and do some wandering:
a third city
          needs to arise
                    on this site,
a third city:
          Red Berlin.
Fight these Goliaths
                    with your slingshots:
break through the bayonets,
                    set the prisoners free.
Last election,
          communists got
                    three million votes:
the first green shoot of recovery!

·1924·

Jubilee

Alexander Sergeievich,* allow me to introduce myself: Mayakovsky.

Give me your hand!
        The cage of my ribs.
                Not beating but moaning:
                        you hear that?
I'm worried about my heart,
                a lion turned into a lapdog.
I never knew my shamefully
            frivolous
                head
contained so many thousand tonnes of crap.
I pull you by the hand.
                I guess I surprised you?
Did I squeeze too hard?
            Did I hurt you?
                    Sorry, my dear.
What's the harm
        in wasting
            an hour or two?
Both you and I
        have eternity to spare.
Let's be like water
           and scurry along chattering,
let's be like spring,
          liberated and unchained!
The moon
        up in the sky
           is so young
it would be risky

---

* This poem addresses Alexander Sergeievich Pushkin, Russia's national poet, the 125th anniversary of whose birth was being celebrated at the time. As a signatory of the 1912 Futurist Manifesto, 'A Slap in the Face of Public Taste', Mayakovsky called for Pushkin to be 'thrown from the steamship of modernity'.

to let her go out
                    on her own.
I am now free
                from love
                        and propaganda.
I'm wearing
            the sharp-clawed bear
                                of jealousy
                                        like a hide.
You can see for yourself
                        that the ground is
sloping:
            sit down on your buttocks
                                    and slide!
No, I'm not wallowing
                    in loathèd melancholy,
but I don't want to take
                        just anybody
                                by the hand.
It's just that
            the gills of rhyme
                            flutter more quickly
on those such as us,
                    cast up on poetry's sand.
Dreams
        can be harmful
                    and dreaming is useless:
you have to carry on your needful toil.
Sometimes you see
                the bigger picture
                                through the rubbish
when life stands up
                at a different angle.
More than once,
                into lyrics,
                        our bayonets we've stúck in:
we look for a speech that is naked,

                        direct.
But poetry's
              an off-the-wall ker-ayzee motherfucker:
It exists,
         it just is,
                  it's a matter of fact.
Look at this
           for example,
                        is it sayable
                                    or bleatable?
A blue face
          with an orange moustache
                            on top,
like Nebuchadnezzar
                 from the Bible:
the logo for a Co-op.
Fill up our glasses! I know it's an old way
to try to drown one's sorrows,
but look!
          the Red and White Star Lines –
                                    anchors aweigh! –
in a gurgle of various visas.
You're alright,
             you are,
                     I'm glad you're here with me.
Your Muse made you a great entertainer.
What was it
           that Olga used to say?
No, not Olga!
            Onegin,
                   writing to Tatiana.
'So,
    your husband's a fool
                      and he can't get it up,
I love you,
          you have to be mine,
I need to be sure
                in the morning

       when I wake up
that I'll see you this afternoon.'
Yeah, there's been a lot of that:
        standing underneath windows,
letters,
   stomach turning to jelly.
But when
   you're not
     even in the mood
       to be sorrowful –
then that,
    Alexander Sergeievich,
       is far less easy.
Let's go, Mayakovsky!
      Make off for the south!
         Let's go!
Squeeze out your heart in rhymes,
       for
love has been knocked out
my dear Vladimir.
No,
  this isn't anything to do
with getting older!
     I can still compel this raddled body,
and I'd be happy
    to fight with two
(or,
  if my dander was up,
     with three).
They say my themes are too
       i-n-d-i-v-i-d-u-a-l-i-s-t-i-c
(*pas devant les enfants,*
     I don't want to be censored completely).
But let me tell you,
    there's a rumour
      that they've even seen
two people
   in love

                        on the Central Executive Committee.
And so,
        they've gossiped
                        and they've amused themselves with it.
Alexander Sergeievich,
                    don't listen to them!
Maybe
        I'm
              the only
                    one
                        who truly regrets
you're no longer around
                        in the world of men.
We should thrash things out
                        while I'm still alive.
Soon
      I'll be
            dead
                  and dumb.
After death
          we'll be close enough
                              to each other:
You under P,
            me under M.
Who's there between us?
                      Who will we have to spend time with?
In this country there are too many
                              crappy
                                    poets.
Between P and M
                there's the appalling Nadson*
                                        to rhyme with.
He should be filed
                somewhere around Z.

---

* Semyon Yakovlevich Nadson (1862–87), sentimental poet.

There's Kolya Nekrasov,*
                    Alyosha's boy,
He plays cards,
              he writes poems,
                          he looks alright.
He'll be company for us,
                    he can stay.
Do you know him?
                He's a good lad.
And what
        about
              my contemporaries
                            (snore)?
It wouldn't be an unfair swap:
                        you for fifty of them.
                                          Oh,
they'll make you yawn so much
                        you'll dislocate your jaw:
Gerasimov,
          Kirillov,
                  Rodov,
                        Dorogoichenko...†
A pretty worthy
              oh so worthy
                          tedious worthy crew!
With his pals
            who pretend
                      to be peasants,
                                there's Yesenin.
Enough to make a cat laugh!

---

* Nikolai Nekrasov (1821–78), poet and publisher, champion of the peasants'
cause in pre-Revolutionary Russia.
† Mikhail Gerasimov (1889–1939), Vladimir Kirillov (1889–1937), Semion
Rodov (1893–1968), Aleksei Dorogoichenko (1894–1947): Russian poets,
Mayakovsky's contemporaries. His assessment of them is fair. Later on in the
poem Mayakovsky mentions Sergey Yesenin (see p.165), Alexander Bezy-
mensky (1898–1973), and Nikolai Aseyev (1889–1963), all poets slightly
more talented than this initial quartet.

Cows in spats.
> Fakers.
A voice from the chorus,
> > if you give him a listen,
Him and his balalaika.
A poet
> needs
> > to be good at life as well.
You and me,
> we're strong
> > as the booze in a Poltava taproom.
What about,
> I dunno,
> > Bezymensky?
> > > Well…
He's like coffee made out of acorns.
We do have Kolya Aseyev, true.
He'll do. He's almost as strong as me.
But we've really got a lot of work to do!
We're small, but we're a family.
You could be
> co-editor of *Lef* *
> > if you were still around.
I'd even
> trust you
> > to do agitprop
> > > material.
I'd show you once,
> so you could see how it's done,
but you'd do fine,
> you write pretty well.
I'd let you do the perfume layout work
To sell perfume and cloth to all the ladies.
(Oh look,

---

* *Lef*, the journal of L E F, the Left Front of the Arts, edited by Mayakovsky and Osip Brik.

I've come over
                    all iambic
to make you feel
                    like this is your place.)
Nowadays
            you'd have to drop
                            this iambic palaver.
Our pens
        are bayonets
                    and pitchforks' tines.
The struggles of the Revolution
                            were more serious than 'Poltava',
and our love
            is more expansive
                        than any of Onegin's.
Be afraid of Pushkinologists.
                            Some addle-brained old Pliushkin,*
holding his little pen is
                        bound to blow his top.
'So, apparently, *Lef* has now got Pushkin.
'That blackamoor!
                    Derzhavin will come out on top.'†
It is you alive,
            and not a mummy,
                        that I love.
Here
    you've been painted
                    with schoolbook varnish.
But I think that you,
            you African,
                        while you lived,
were also loud
        and riotous!

---

* Stepan Pliushkin, a character from Gogol's novel *Dead Souls* (1842), the archetype of the miser, the hoarder of irrelevant details.
† Gavril Derzhavin (1743–1816), the greatest Russian poet before Pushkin.

D'Anthès, son of a bitch!*
　　　　　　　　　That *beau-monde* villain.
'So, what class do your parents belong to?'
　　　　　　　　　　　　　　we'd have asked him.
And also
　　　　　'What did you do before the Revolution?'
If only we'd got
　　　　　　five minutes
　　　　　　　　　alone in the dark with him...
But what's all this nonsense!
　　　　　　　　　It's like a fricking séance.
To summarise:
　　　　　　a prisoner of honour,
　　　　　　　　　　　　shot down cruelly...
There are still
　　　　　all kinds of people
　　　　　　　　　who chase other men's
wives:
　　　　lots of d'Anthès's sort
　　　　　　　　around today.
We're doing pretty well
　　　　　　　in this Soviet country.
We can live,
　　　　　we can work
　　　　　　　　in a comradely fashion.
But,
　　well,
　　　　　as for poets,
　　　　　　　　it's a shame,
　　　　　　　　　　　but there aren't any –
but maybe poets aren't really an obligation.
Anyway,
　　　　time to go:
　　　　　　　the sun's rays are burning hard.

---

* Georges-Charles de Heeckeren d'Anthès (1812–1895), French politician
and soldier. He killed Pushkin in a duel in 1837.

The police
                are going
                            to put out
                                        an all-points call.
People are used to you,
                            here on Tverskoy Boulevard.
Come on,
            let's get you back on your pedestal.
I reckon
            by now
                        I'm entitled to a monument.
I'd fill it with dynamite and…
                                        piff!
                                              Paff!
                                                    Puff!
I hate everything that's dead and spent!
I love everything that's filled with life!

·1924·

Hooliganish Stuff

Scarcely
       has the sun set,
              sinking
behind
      an empty
           factory,
than the suburbs
         groan
              with hooligans:
like this pleasant group
          of three.
You're walking along
           and there they are,
a little way off.
          You'll have a run-in tonight.
There's no way out,
         there's no way past,
not for woman
       or man
          or streetlight.
'Hey little lady,
        don't run away,
             come for a walk…
A club?
     Why?
        Break the chairs!
He's making problems?
           A knife in the back!
Knock out their teeth,
        break their jaws!'
With beer fumes
       buzzing
          in their heads,

their tiny thoughts
                    jumbled up
                                with homebrew,
it's not
        with weapons
                    the air is filled,
but with language
                turning the air blue.
Workers,
        for this
                    we gave the blood from our veins?
Is this what you want
                    for your daughters?
While it's not too late,
                        put an end
to this intrusive
                and ugly ulcer!

·1924·

Brooklyn Bridge

Hey, Coolidge!
Nice bridge!
Credit
      where credit's due.
Blush as red
         as the Soviet flag
Though you're from the disU-
Nited States of America.

Like a believer,
        a monk from his cell
Starting out
      on a pilgrimage
I,
  as the evening
       begins to fall,
Step onto
     Brooklyn Bridge.
Like a great conqueror,
         drunk on victory,
Who forces
     his cannon
        into the breach
Or marches
     triumphant
        to a ruined city
So I set foot
     on Brooklyn Bridge.
As a foolish
     painter
       will fall in love
If he stares
    too long
       at some pouting
          artwork
So I,

          glaring down from high above,
Fall
      from the Brooklyn Bridge
                        for New York.
New York,
           by day so funky and oppressive
Forgets
        to be hard
               and heavy
                    by night –
Here and there
             an occasional house-elf
Silhouetted in a square of light.
And far away,
           the elevated trains
With their clink
          and rattle –
                 like clearing a table.
From up here,
          ships' masts
               look like pins;
The ships themselves,
                like sugar mills.
I am proud
        of this steel mile,
Here, my visions can stand up straight.
This is function
             instead of style:
A strict provision
             of rivets and weight.
If chaos comes
           and gives us a knock,
Smashes
      this planet
             into broken bits
Even then,
       above
          the havoc

This will remain –
                the Brooklyn Bridge.
And then,
          like tiny
               vertebrae
Are extrapolated into dinosaurs,
A geologist
              from some future
                       century
Will recreate this world of ours.
He will say,
              'This tongue of steel
'Once stretched
              from here
                    to the Wild West,
'And linked
             the ocean
                   to the dustbowl,
'Tore the beads
              from an Indian headdress.
'The arc
         of the bridge
                 is like
                    a fishing rod –
'Do you think,
              if you could get a hook in,
'And braced yourself
               on the Manhattan side,
'And yanked
          hard enough,
                    you'd reel in Brooklyn?
'By analysis
          of these wires and cables
'I date
        this bridge
              back to Modern times:
'Days with a radio
            on every table,

'Days when mankind
                    was learning to fly...
'Then,
        some people
                  had life easier.
'For most,
          life was a stretched-out
                               shout of pain.
'From this bridge,
                 there leapt
                            to the river
'Hordes
       of hungry
                and jobless
                           men.
'And I can postulate further,
'From these strands
                   against
                          the apocalyptic sky:
'Here,
      the presence
                  of our great forefather
'Vladimir
         Vladimirovich
                      Mayakovsky.'
I gawp
      like a caveman
                   scratching
                             his brow-ridge.
I burrow my way
               into this structure
                                  like a flea.
Brooklyn Bridge –
Fuck me!

·1925·

To Sergei Yesenin*

As the phrase has it,
                you've passed over.
Emptiness…
        fly on,
                carving your name on the night sky.
No more advances,
             no more beer.
Sobriety.
No,
    Yesenin,
           this isn't a joke.
Grief lumpish in my throat,
                I'm not taking the piss.
I see you swinging
           the bag
                of your own bones,
calling a halt to it all
                by cutting your wrists.
Stop it!
      That's enough!
                Are you crazy?
To let
      your cheeks
            be sicklied o'er
                    with the chalk of death?
You,
    who could talk
           a blue streak of poetry

* Sergei Yesenin, a popular poet, the object of a certain amount of respectful mockery from Mayakovsky throughout his life, killed himself in the Hotel Angleterre, Saint Petersburg, on 28 December 1925. His final poem, written in his own blood and found by his body, ends with the lines 'В этой жизни умирать не ново, / Но и жить, конечно, не новей' (In this life it is not new to die, / but living, of course, is not any newer), which Mayakovsky riffs on at the end of his elegy.

like no one else on earth.
Why?
        Why did you do it?
                        It weighs on us, our incomprehension.
The critics grumble:
                'It must be due to this,
                                or that,
                                        or this,
                                                or…
the most important factor,
                a lack of real connection,
which led
        to too much
                wine and beer.'
I think they mean
                that if you'd abandoned
                                the bohemian class
you'd have shaken
                its influence
                        and felt no need to fight.
But there's no shortage
                of drinkers
                        among the workers:
what do you think they drink?
                        Coca-Cola?
                                        Sprite?
They say,
        you could have written
                        in a really gifted way
had you been partnered
                with a true
                        proletarian.
You'd have produced
                a hundred lines a day
Lengthy
        and boring

as something by Doronin.*
If you'd gone in
            for any of that crap
                        they propose,
you'd have slit your wrists sooner,
                        deeper,
                              and more often.
Better it is to die from booze
than to die from boredom!
The reasons
            for this loss
                        will not be revealed either
by the noose
            or by that little knife
                        for sharpening pens.
Maybe if there'd been
                  any ink
                        in the Hotel Angleterre,
there'd have been no reason
                        for you to cut your veins.
Your imitators were happy:
                  'Encore! Encore!'
A platoon of them
            have killed themselves!
                        ('¡*Que viva el* groupthink!')
Why do they increase
                  the suicide figures?
Better to increase
                  the production of ink!
Behind your teeth
            your tongue now
                        is forever locked.

---

* Ivan Ivanovich Doronin (1900–78), Soviet poet, author of such attractive tomes as *Songs of the Soviet Fields* (1924), *The Tractor Driver* (1926) and *What Songs the People of the Fatherland Sing* (1968).

It would be hard
                    and inappropriate
                                        to foment mystery.
Let's just say that for the people,
                                for the makars,
a resonant
            profligate
                        apprentice-in-language
                                            has died.
And they bring
                their scraps
                            of eulogistic balladry,
barely altered
                from their use
                                at previous funerals.
Is this really
                how we want
                            to fix a poet
                                        in our memory:
by using a stick
                and driving dull rhymes uphill?
They've not yet
                put up your monument –
what'll it be?
                Granular granite
                                or sounding brass? –
but already
            they've brought
                            to the mausoleum
the filth
        of dedications
                        and reminiscences.
And your name was snivelled in hankies,
and Sóbinov* sobbed out your words;

* Leonid Vitalyevich Sobinov (1872–1934), popular Russian (later Soviet)
tenor.

he stood in a thicket of birches
and sang so he frightened the birds:
'No words, my friend, no sigh-igh-íng.'
(He should have stuck to Lohengrin.)
Oh, I'd have loved
          to cause
                   a thundering scandal:
'I won't let you mumble
              and rumble
                    his poems!'
I'd have deafened them
              with a two-fingered whistle
and told them
          to go to h…
              to go home.
I wish
     I'd got rid
          of those talentless shits,
tempesting away
          their jacket-sails' darkness;
I'd have made Kogan* run off
              like a cat with the squits,
maiming passers-by
          with his moustaches.
Meanwhile
        we need
           to weed out
              the trash.
There's a lot to do,
          and speed is everything.
We need
     to remake
         life
           from scratch;

---

* Piotr Semionovich Kogan (1873–1932), literary critic. In his essay 'How to Make a Poem' (1926), Mayakovsky is critical of Kogan's approach to Yesenin. Judging by the surviving photographs, Kogan's moustaches could indeed have been used as deadly weapons.

once it's remade,
                then we can start to sing.
This is a
       schlechte
          Zeit
             für Lyrik,
but tell me,
        cripples great and small,
when
     and where
          did a great man ever take
the well-trodden path
            where there was no chance he'd fall?
The human forces:
         the word
            is their commander.
Marchons!
       Let time
          explode like bombs behind us.
Let it be
     no more
         than a tangle
            of hair
that the wind
       carries back
          to the olden days.
Our planet
      is poorly set up
         for joy.
We have to rip pleasure
          from what the future brings.
In this life
      it is not hard to die.
To make a life
       is by far the harder thing.

·1926·

How's It Going?*

A Day in Five Cine-Details

Prologue

1. A street. A normal guy is walking along: Mayakovsky. Panorama.
2. Panorama from the other side. The guy keeps on walking against the same background, the same buildings.
3. People.
4. Cars.
5. Trams.
6. Buses. (*Shots 3–6 are the background to the stroll.*)
7. Another guy walking along, almost identical.
8. He walks almost the same way, rubbing his hands like a mill grinding.
9. Hands.
10. Shots 1–6.
11. The first normal guy walks along.
12. The second normal guy walks along.
13. The first normal guy walks along.
14. The second normal guy walks along. (*The montage mixes together here, to prepare for the meeting.*)
15. Mayakovsky stops, looks around, starts to rub his hands and walks on.
16. The second Mayakovsky sees him, pauses, looks around, walks on.
17. The hands of the first Mayakovsky rubbing together.
18. The hands of the second Mayakovsky rubbing together.
19. The hands strike together, streams of water shoot out from between the palms in all directions.
20. Both stand with clenched hands, motionless, like in provincial photographs. They stay still for a long time. (*Like a photograph.*) The background movement is increased and prolonged.

---

* An unfilmed screenplay.

21. The first one twists his immobile face into a smile using only his lips. (*Like the actor Tikhomorov.*)
22. The second one twists his immobile face into a smile using only his lips.
23. The first one seizes the second one's hand.
24. The second one seizes the first one's hand.
25. The first one doffs his hat.
26. The second one doffs his hat.
27. The first one takes off his collar out of sheer joy.
28. The second one takes off his moustache.
29. Both of them have an expression of the purest pleasure. Out of one mouth comes the letter 'H'. Immediately, the words 'How's it going?' come out of the other's mouth.

How's It Going?

30. They come close to each other, face to face, and staring intently at each other, wait for an answer.
31. Both of them suddenly walk to the sides of the frame. They stretch out a hand towards the other.
32. Between the tips of the stretched-out hands appears the following:

Part One
Everybody, apart from the rich and the dead,
greets the morning like this:

33. A black screen. The following drawings appear done in chalk: an old woman drinks coffee; the coffee pot turns into a cat. The cat plays with a ball of wool, zigzag arrows come out of the ball of wool and point to the face of the sleeping Mayakovsky. (*He materialises through the outlines of the sketch*)
34. A bed. Mayakovsky in the bed. The background behind the bed transforms into the sea.
35. The sea. Half of the sun on the horizon.
36. The sun is covered with clouds. A single ray of light shines through the clouds.
37. On the black screen a beam of light, steadily intensifying, that starts thin at the window and gradually widens as it reaches

the bed.

38. In the beam of light are clearly visible fragments of the sleeping man.

39. Pedestrians appear in the ray of light, wandering around and walking away.

40. Footsteps.

41. The bed shakes because of the footsteps.

42. The man shifts over onto his side.

43–50. Cars and vans appear one by one in the beam of light, all laden with food.

51. The bed shakes even more. The man shifts over onto his other side.

52–55. Into the ray of light appears all the hubbub of the city: trams, cars, trucks, pedestrians.

56. The man thrashes about from side to side.

57–61. Mingling with one another, the sounds of car horns, tram bells, steamship whistles and factory sirens.

62. It is bright in the room. The man half opens his eyes and brings his watch to his face. It shows a quarter to eight.

63. The minute and the second hands of the watch are close to the upper and lower eyelids of the man. As the hands move apart, so the man's eyes open. (*All of the movements of the watch-hands should be entirely realistic, and the watch-face should only move a tiny bit when the hands move*)

64. The man jumps up, opens his door a little way and shouts into the crack.

65. The view through the crack. Mayakovsky's room. The following letters comes out of his mouth:

'N e w s p a p e r !'

66. One by one the letters move around the room and then down the corridor, then they rush into the kitchen and one by one they reach the head of the cook, who is sitting by the samovar, and disappear into it.

67. Mayakovsky plugs in the electric kettle.

68–69. The cook gets up and slides down the stairs.

70. The man walks around the room, rubbing his face with his hands.

71. The cook stops in front of a newspaper kiosk.

The World on Paper

72. The newsagent gives the cook several newspapers.

73. The cook slings the basket of food, crowned with the newspapers, over her right shoulder. She walks off.

74. Two Young Communists stop by the newspaper kiosk. They pick up a newspaper. They glance through it, looking for the short lines of poems. They wring their hands.

'No poems again. What a boring newspaper.'

75–80. The cook is walking along. The newspapers over her shoulder grow bigger, they bend her over towards the ground. The houses that the cook is walking in front of grow smaller. The cook shrinks as well. The houses shrink as well. The cook is carrying a huge globe on her shoulders. She walks and can barely move her legs because of the weight.

81. The street in perspective. The tramlines. In the distance appears a large globe rolling along the tramlines, and rapidly getting bigger.

82. The entrance to the house. The door to the staircase opens by itself. The globe rolls up to the door. It shrinks until it can get through the door.

83. Having rolled through the door, it rolls up the steps by itself.

84. The door to the flat with a plaque: 'Brik. Mayakovsky.' The cook walks through the door carrying her shopping and the newspapers.

85–86. The newspapers come through the crack in the door to where Mayakovsky is rinsing his razor. He picks one up and sits at his chair.

87. Mayakovsky moves his head, looks.

88. The writing desk.

89. A radio mast.

90. Mayakovsky looks over a page of the newspaper.

91. Out of the newspaper comes a train.

92–93. Details of the workings of a steam engine.

94. Mayakovsky moves slightly away from the newspaper.

95. An aeroplane flies out.

96–97. Details of the workings of an aeroplane.

98. Mayakovsky at his desk. He unfolds the paper completely.

99. Mayakovsky's eye.

100. A detail of the newspaper: the leading article *Our Export Is Bread*.

101. At the edge of the leading article appears the cartoon of a person wearing pince-nez, and, leaning against the edge of the newspaper like a lectern, he pushes himself out into the room.

102. He takes Mayakovsky's hand, shakes it very forcefully and then starts talking. Facts and figures pour our of his mouth.

103. The figures pour into Mayakovsky's ear, swirl round his head.

104–106. Mayakovsky starts to fidget, move around in his chair, say to himself, 'we know all this, it's obvious'. Finally he puts a calm and peaceful hand on the leading article's shoulder and pushes him back into the newspaper.

107. Mayakovsky turns the page. He carries on reading.

108. Mayakovsky's eyes open wide; he throws himself down into an armchair and looks around the room.

109. All the objects on the writing desk start to move.

110. The lamp falls over.

111. The calendar shifts to a different page. There are bits of newspaper type left on the table, forming the phrase, *Earthquake in Leningrad*. The man looks closely at the fragments of newspaper on the table; his hands and his shoulders are shaking. He listens carefully.

112. He turns round.

113. The kettle is boiling.

114. Mayakovsky takes the kettle and puts it among the scraps of newspaper on the table. The kettle whistles, shakes, struggles as if there were an active volcano inside it. The man looks at the boiling water, smiles, takes the scraps of newspaper. They become a normal page from a newspaper once again.

115. Mayakovsky continues reading.

116. *The growth of bureaucra...* a head with a pen behind its ear appears from out of the last 'a'. It becomes a figure who puts his hands on the border of the newspaper, pulls himself out of the page, grows larger and starts to wave pens and pencils.

117. Mayakovsky stands in front of this apparition, then struggles with it, grabs it by the throat, strangles it and pushes it with

difficulty back into the page.

118–119. Mayakovsky takes a gulp of tea, blows on the cup and swallows, then sees: *In Brief.* One of the articles attracts his attention.

120. He sits down, breathes heavily. He adjusts his tie. He reads.

121. *A suicide... yesterday at 6 PM, twenty-two years old, single gunshot... a hopeless situa...*

122. The newspaper stands up and moves into the corner, becomes a kind of screen.

123. A young woman appears from out of the dark screen, in despair, holding a revolver in one hand. She puts the revolver to her temple and pulls the trigger.

124. Bursting through the newspaper like a dog in a circus jumping through a paper hoop, Mayakovsky rushes into the room that appears in the newspaper / screen.

125. He tries to grab the revolver from the girl's hand, but he is too late. The girl falls to the floor.

126. Mayakovsky takes a step back. His face is horrorstricken.

127. Mayakovsky in his room again. He takes the newspaper, carefully puts his tea to one side and throws the newspaper down on the table.

128. His face gradually calms down. He looks at the newspaper again.

129. *Advertisements.*

Get your clothes made and your sewing done in Moscosew shops.

130. An overcoat hangs in the corner. There is stuffing coming out of its lining. The collar is ripped. Mayakovsky lifts it up with two fingers and looks out through the holes in it.

131. *Advertisements. Get your clothes made...* The street. Along the street glide crumpled, nocturnal, independent items of clothing with no people inside them: overcoats and suits, trousers, jackets and waistcoats, and each of them has a price where the head would normally appear.

132. Just the prices, flashing.

133. Mayakovsky thoughtfully bites his lips, and makes sums on his fingers.

134. The flashing prices slide together and add themselves up and

become a large sum.

135. The number turns into a bag of coins.

136. The bag of coins jangles in front of his face.

137. The man stands up and looks at the bag thoughtfully.

138. A book of poems appears before his face next to the bag of coins. The book falls open and new books grow out of it.

139. Two pens appear between the bag of coins and the books of poems, looking like an equals sign.

140. Mayakovsky takes one of the pens.

<u>You have to work.</u>
End of Part One

Part Two

1. The man stands by the window, sharpening a pencil with a razor blade.

2. He holds the pen up to the window and brandishes it.

Give me poems!

3. A piggish family is sitting at a tea table.

4. The clean-shaven father appears in the centre of the screen.

I don't need poems.

5. A Young Communist with his Young Communist sweetheart under the moon. The girl pulls back from her boyfriend, mentally begging:

Give us poems!

6. The paterfamilias's collar falls down, but then his beard grows and covers the glass of tea that he holds in his hand.

I don't need poems.

7. The Young Communist in front of the newsagent's:

Give us poems!

8. The paterfamilias turns into a monkey before our eyes.

I don't need your poems.

9. A poster. A poetry fight: Aseyev, Kirsanov, Mayakovsky, Pasternak.*

---

* Aseyev (see note on p. 154); Semion Kirsanov (pseudonym of Semion Kortchik (1906–1972), Futurist poet; Boris Pasternak (1890–1960), poet and novelist, winner of the 1958 Nobel Prize for Literature.

10. The hall in a worker's social club, full to the brim and applauding.

11. Mayakovsky standing still and looking around him.

12. Mayakovsky decisively rolls up his sleeves.

13. Mayakovsky sucks on his pencil.

14. Mayakovsky strikes his pencil against the paper. A factory with no smoke or chimneys.

15. He wipes his forehead. His hands shudder like someone getting an electric shock.

16. Words start to pour out of his head and move around the room.

17. Mayakovsky runs around, skewering the words on his pencil.

18. Mayakovsky pulls the words off the end of the pencil like bagels off a pole, and pins them with difficulty down on the page.

19. The flying words pull themselves out of half-formed phrases and fly off again.

20. Phrases such as 'How beautiful, how fresh the roses were' and 'the bird knows no master' stay on the page for a short while.

21. Mayakovsky divides the words with his pencil, and separates and chooses the ones he needs.

22. They settle on the page again.

23. Mayakovsky rejoices in what he has written.

24. The words on the page make up the phrase 'Left, left, left!'

25. Mayakovsky standing next to the window with a sharpened pencil, smiling and decided.

26. He gathers the pencil shavings onto a piece of newspaper and throws them out of the window. A fan spins in the window.

27. He takes a sheet of paper out of the desk and looks at it lovingly.

28. The fan spins.

29. The fan pulls the bad rhymes out of the poem: blood – mud – dud, free – me, son – sun &c.

30. Mayakovsky works over the manuscript again, then signs it and stands up happily.

31. Happily he rolls up the page into a tube and ties it with a ribbon, then

32. goes downstairs without touching the steps. (*This is the old*

phrase, 'he was walking on air'.)

33–35. He goes down the street, making huge steps and hardly moving his legs. He is at least two heads taller than everyone else in the street. The other pedestrians turn to look at him. The wind lifts up the tails of his overcoat and makes him look like a demon.

36. Mayakovsky in the editor's waiting room. Next to Mayakovsky sit a whole line of other people with similarly tied-up sheets of paper, obviously a whole series of other people waiting for meetings.

37. Mayakovsky's name is called.

38. Mayakovsky goes into the editor's office. He hits against the doorframe as he comes in and breaks it in half.

39. Mayakovsky and the editor shake hands. Mayakovsky shrinks down to the same size as the editor. The editor is a newspaper bureaucrat. He invites Mayakovsky to read.

40–42. Starting at the same size as the poet the editor shrinks and shrinks, becoming very small. Mayakovsky offers him the manuscript, which has grown to gigantic proportions, four times as big as the editor. A tiny chess piece is sitting at the editor's desk.

43. The poet reads in an auditorium.

44. The editor, once he has heard the poem, twists in his chair, looks at the manuscript again, makes an angry face and turns on the poet. Mayakovsky becomes small. The editor becomes huge, four times the size of the poet. The poet becomes a little chess piece on the edge of the chair.

45. The monkey family is in the background as the editor speaks.

46. The poet picks up a piece of paper that says *Invoice.*

47. The poet comes back at the editor bravely, growing in stature again, but not as much as before.

48. Behind the poet, a group of Young Communists.

49. The editor grows to a gigantic size. The little poet Mayakovsky stands on the chair; the editor holds out a contract.

50. Happy monkeys behind the editor.

51. The editor writes *10 roubles advance.*

52. Mayakovsky leaves the office, small, scarcely visible over the threshold.

53. The poet stands in a queue at the cash desk.

54. A sign at the cash desk: *The cashier will return.*

55. The poet starts to yawn.

56. The poet starts to feel sleepy.

57. The grille in front of the cash desk becomes a flower-covered trellis from a southern garden.

58. The fan on the desk turns into a bird.

59. As he falls asleep he knocks over an inkstand. Ink flows all over the papers.

60–61. The pages flow off the desk and run together and become the real Black Sea.

62. Palm trees wave in the wind.

63. Palm leaves rub against the poet's nose.

64. Mayakovsky wakes up. The cleaner's feather-duster is tickling his nose.

What are you doing asleep? The cashier won't come back today, you come back on Wednesday.

65. Mayakovsky walks down the street. He looks around.

66. The window of *Moscosew.*

67. Mayakovsky takes his watch out of his waistcoat pocket and looks at it. Five thirty. The hands are pointing in the same direction. He puts it back in his pocket.

68. It feels as if the hands of the watch are poking into his stomach. He walks along led by his stomach.

69. Mayakovsky stops in front of a bakery window, then takes his small change out of his pocket and counts it.

70–72. Mayakovsky goes into the shop and looks at the prices, then buys a little package of food. Bread and sausage.

End of Part Two

Part Three
Our Daily Bread

1. Mayakovsky sits at his table in his room, chewing something with no pleasure or interest, flicking through the newspaper. He picks up a piece of bread in one hand, holds it up to his mouth, doesn't bite it, looks at it with distaste, then frowns and throws it back on the table.

So much work just for a piece of bread!
2. The unbitten piece of bread falls onto the floor.
3. The leading-article man climbs out of the newspaper again, takes Mayakovsky by his hand and points at the floor.
All that work for this piece of bread!
4. The crust of bread lying on the floor.
5. The crust of bread jumps back into Mayakovsky's hand.
6. The bread he has already eaten climbs out of Mayakovsky's mouth and heads back to the bread.
7. He puts the bread back on the table, the piece of bread joins the rest of the loaf.
8. The man climbs into his jacket and walks backwards to the door.
9. The man goes down the stairs backwards.
10. The man walks along the street.
11. The man goes into the shop.
12. The man gives the bread back.
13. The man backs over to the cash desk.
14. They pay the man at the cash desk.
15. He leaves the shop.
16. The bread jumps back onto the shelf.
17. The bread jumps off the shelf into a box of bread.
18. The bread jumps into the oven.
19. The bread becomes dough.
20. The dough turns back into flour.
21. The flour returns to a sack.
22. People carry the sack to the back entrance of the bakery, to a truck.
23. They load the sack onto the truck.
24. The label is taken off the sack.
25. The label returns to a heap of papers.
26. The heap of papers is packed into a box.
27. The box is stacked together with other boxes.
28. The boxes are loaded into a car.
29. The car backs to the paper factory.
30. The trucks filled with bags of flour return to the mill.
31. They accept the flour into the mill.
32. The flour is poured into the mill.

33. The mill turns the flour into grain.
34. The grain is gathered into bags by peasants.
35. The peasants take the bags to the threshing floor.
36. The bags are emptied and threshed back into stalks of wheat.
37. The stalks of wheat are tied together into bundles.
38. The bundles are carried back to the field.
39. The threshing machine backs away over the field.
40. The girl from the *In Brief* section walks hand-in-hand across the field with Mayakovsky.
41. The wheat starts to grow smaller.
42. The wheat turns into green shoots.
43. The ground is ploughed.
44. The furrows in the ground grow smaller.
45. The peasants disappear.
46. They are chased out of the village.
47–49. The attacked, burnt village.
50–52. The partisans repel an attack.
53. The city filled with demonstrating crowds.
54–56. All the placards and posters carried by the demonstrators read *Bread and Peace*. This becomes a diagram.
57. Mayakovsky appears out of the diagram in his room, holding his glass of tea and with the crust of bread still on the floor.
58. The man from the leading article shakes his hand and disappears back into the newspaper.
59. Mayakovsky looks at the bread on the floor.
60. Mayakovsky carefully picks up the crust.
61. Mayakovsky shakes the dust off the bread.
62. Mayakovsky puts the crust into a battered but expensive bowl. He cleans the bowl with his jacket and covers the bread up with his own handkerchief. He walks away, musing to himself.

End of Part Three

Part Four
Natural Love
Stone
1. A few normal peaceful stones.
Mud

2. Normal peaceful mud.

Action

3. A hand takes a stone.

4. The stone is thrown into the mud.

Result

5. Circular stains of mud on the screen.

People

6–8. A candle is lit in a room, the candle is carried by a porter, a room appears behind the porter.

9–11. Another room. The guests at the wedding are welcomed.

Event

12. A house is on fire.

13–15. The fire brigade arrive.

16–17. People run out of the house.

18–20. People surround the house in crowds.

21–24. People dressed for a celebration come out of various flats, reading congratulatory messages for the wedding.

25–28. People run out of the house.

29–32. The bride and groom sit in a horse-drawn carriage.

33–35. People in carriages and cars follow the wedding procession. Pedestrians catch up with the carriage.

36. The house of the couple.

37. People keep on arriving and looking through the windows.

38. The guests arrive.

39. The city from above.

40–41. The crowd of people outside the burning house.

42–43. The crowd of people outside the house of the married couple.

One of the crowds

44. The crowd outside the wedding: in the middle of the crowd, a young woman hurrying and obviously worrying about something.

One of the crowds

45. The crowd by the burning building: in the middle of the crowd, Mayakovsky looking around and obviously worrying about something.

The crowds meet each other

46–47. The two circles, one part surrounding the woman, the

other part surrounding Mayakovsky.

48–49. The two circles combine into one.

50. The young woman looks at Mayakovsky. Mayakovsky looks at the young woman from his half of the circle. She's a woman, all right.

51. The woman leaves her part of the circle.

52. Mayakovsky leaves his part of the circle.

53. Mayakovsky hurries towards the woman. He looks at her. In his eyes she becomes the woman from the *In Brief* section.

54. He scolds her.

> *I'm not going to talk to you.*

55. The woman takes a step back, shakes her head a few times, then decisively nods.

56. Finally they get into conversation.

> *I'm not going to go anywhere with you, just stroll a little bit.*

57. They take a couple of steps together.

58. Then they take each other's arms and walk together.

59–61. Mayakovsky kicks an abandoned flower off the edge of the pavement.

62. Mayakovsky stops outside the door to his house.

> *Don't come in with me, just for a minute.*

63–69. It is winter everywhere, but in front of the house is a garden in flower, trees with birds in them: the façade of the house is entirely covered in roses. The porter in his heavy overcoat wipes away the sweat that is running down his face.

> *On the wings of love.*

70–72. The woman and Mayakovsky grow aeroplane wings.

73–74. The woman and Mayakovsky fly up the staircase.

75–80. Everything in the dirty room lights up; lilies grow in the inkwell, the wallpaper pattern transforms into a pattern of little roses. The simple lamp becomes a chandelier.

81. Mayakovsky runs some water out of the tap.

> *We won't drink, just a glass.*

82. The woman speaks:

> *Your water is very strong!*

83–84. He takes the glass from her hands and starts to move towards her.

We won't kiss!

85. Their lips reach out towards each other.

86–89. The façade of the house, the flowers are flying off the wall, there is still snow in the street. The doorman in his shirtsleeves hurries to get back into his fur coat.

90–93. The room, returned to its normal dirty appearance.

94–96. They come out of the entrance. He's wearing boots, she's in worn-down heels. They're carrying their wings tucked under their arms. They slip. They yawn.

97. After taking a few paces, Mayakovsky looks at his watch.

98–101. It's twenty-two minutes past nine. The hands are pointing in different directions. The man points in the direction of the hour hand and says goodbye. They go off in different directions.

End of Part Four

Part Five
Day and Night

1–11. The work of the central reservoir. A huge amount of water pours out of the filters. The veins of the pipeline. The main line.

People who use water

12. The camera follows a pipeline.

13. A kitchen. Mayakovsky pours water into a samovar.

Positions of power

14–16. A kitchen. A policeman flirts with the cook. He takes off his uniform jacket.

17–18. Mayakovsky fans the samovar with his socks.

Day and night

19–27. The central telephone exchange. The unceasing work of the telephone operators. Their tangled wires.

Telephone pests

28. An unprepossessing mother talks into a telephone. A father stands behind her in the queue, and then a very tall daughter, three little boys, and two dogs. The telephone conversation.

Just by chance, we'll be round in your area on the eve of Robespierre's birthday.

29. Mayakovsky puts on a loving face and says:

> *Excellent! I'll put the samovar on.*

30. Mayakovsky hangs up, screws up his face and mutters angrily:

> *We'll drink tea when you're gone…*

31–33. The whole family in the street.

34–35. Mayakovsky fans the samovar with his socks: it won't heat up; he looks at his watch. He stops fanning the samovar and puts his socks on, then takes a pair of army boots and starts to put them on.

36. The telephone.

37. Someone calls from the workers' social club.

38. A crowd fills the auditorium.

39. Mayakovsky talking on the phone:

> *I'll come if I can get away.*

40. A ring at the doorbell.

41–42. The family comes in, along with their dogs.

43–45. Mayakovsky invites his guests to sit down, a fixed smile on his face.

46–47. Mayakovsky brings tea to the seated guests.

48–50. The seated guests ask all kinds of questions:

> *Father: is it true that the market in pork bellies is volatile again?*
>
> *Daughter: Tell me, have you ever felt an ideal love?*

51. One of the little boys comes up with his dog:

> *My dog is vewy well-behaved: she pitheth not when she wanth, but when I want.*

52. The mother with pride:

> *My Toto, isn't it true, darling, that he's very big for his age?*

53–55. Mayakovsky answers each of them politely, but as soon as his interlocutor turns away he makes a despairing grimace.

56. The auditorium, filled to the rafters.

57. Three worker's social club committee members on the telephone.

58. Mayakovsky on the telephone.

> *I've got guests.*

59. The guests have finished their tea.

60. Mayakovsky stands up, joyfully rubbing his hands.

61–63. The guests say thank you. But they still stay sitting on the sofa, saying:

It's so nice to come and see you, it's so good to relax.

64. The auditorium, even more full.

65. The telephone rings.

66. Mayakovsky jerks upright at the noise.

67. Mayakovsky runs out of the room.

68. Mayakovsky howls in the kitchen, throwing himself over the kitchen table.

69. Mayakovsky lifts his head up.

70. The policeman's jacket is hanging on a nail: he's obviously staying the night.

71. The happy guests on the sofa.

72. A policeman with a big moustache comes in. He's holding a piece of paper.

Official Orders

73. The worried guests take the paper and read.

An order from the household management. The seismography department. In view of the possibility of the repetition in Moscow of the kind of mild seismic event that recently took place in Leningrad, it is suggested that all inhabitants should spend the night outside of their houses, in the streets. Support this initiative!

74–76. The policeman holds out the paper. Immediately, putting their hats on backwards, their arms in the wrong sleeves of their overcoats, like a family of sheep, they run out, pulling their dogs out by the tails.

77. The husband says worriedly to his wife:

We should say goodbye to our host…

78. The wife pulls at his jacket:

We'll say goodbye tomorrow!

79. Mayakovsky looks around, takes off the moustache and the jacket, and bursts out laughing.

80. He thankfully pulls three roubles out of his trouser pocket.

81. Mayakovsky rushes down the stairs to a taxi.

82. Mayakovsky's journey across town.

83. Mayakovsky onstage.

84. People who talk are thrown out.

85. People who sleep are thrown out.

86. People throw themselves at Mayakovsky.

87. People who grab hold of him are thrown out.
88. Mayakovsky has finished reading. Notes with requests are passed through the auditorium.
89. Applause.
90. An exhausted Mayakovsky heads down the stairs.
91. Mayakovsky's journey across town.
92. Mayakovsky bursts into his room.
93. Mayakovsky sits on his bed and takes off his boots.
94. Mayakovsky tucked up in bed with a book.
95. The room grows blurry.
96. One day it will be like this.
97. A man dictates into a microphone.
98. The auditorium, filled with people listening to a loudspeaker.
99. Notes with requests are sent via telegraph and vacuum tube. It gets dark.
100. It gets darker.
101. Blackness.
102. The family in the middle of a field, shivering under an umbrella.
103. Stars.
104. Mayakovsky is asleep.
105. A dream.
106. The sun rises out of the sea.

The End

·1926·

Conversation with the Taxman about Poetry

Comrade taxman!
                    Do you have a moment?
Thanks...
            don't worry...
                            no, I'll stand...
I'd like
        to talk
                about something quite important:
the poet's position
                    in the economic plan.
You should
            assess me
                    as if
                            I were a shopkeeper
and punish me
                as if
                    that's what I were:
i.e.
    five hundred roubles
                            for this financial quarter
and twenty-five
                for failure to declare.
A poet's job
            is like any other function:
look,
    here's how much
                    my business
                                lost;
here's
    what I laid out
                    on production;
here's
    what
        the raw materials cost.
Of course,

you know
            what I mean
                        by 'rhyme':
you take a word,
            for example,
                        'Mayakovsky'
then repeat
            its sound
                        after leaving
                                    a line
and write,
            as it might be,
                        'sounds off-key'.
To put it
            your way,
                        a rhyme's an I O U
that comes due
            a line –
                        that's the guarantee.
The poet looks
            for something
                        that rings true
in the
      emptying
                  cash-box
                              of his vocabulary.
You stuff
            some particular
                        word in a line
and it won't fit –
            the line buckles
                        and breaks.
Take my word for it,
                        comrade taxman,
it costs
            a lot
                  to keep words in their place.

To put it our way,
                    a rhyme is a box –
a box of dynamite –
                    the line's the fusewire.
The line burns up,
                    the rhyme goes off
and a city's destroyed
                    by a stanza.
Where
        will we find,
                    and with
                            what yield,
rhymes
        that always hit
                    the bull?
Perhaps
        there's a handful
                    left in the wild,
somewhere in the Venezuelan jungle.
So I
        must journey
                in the cold
                        and the heat
asking for advances
                and taking heavy loans:
comrade,
        look how much
                    I spend
                        on transport!
Poetry's
        a voyage
                into
                    the unknown.
Writing
        is like
                extracting radium:

one gram
            to show
                        for the work
                                    of a year.
And in order
            to get to
                        each word,
                                    each gram,
you crush
            a thousand tonnes
                        of verbal ore.
But look
            how brightly
                        these words burn
compared
            to those ones
                        that sputter and fail.
Over the course
            of a thousand years,
these words
            inspire millions
                        and millions
                                    of people.
Of course,
            there are many
                        different kinds of poet.
So many
            of them
                        with their quick,
                                    light fingers...
They conjure up
            lines
                        from their open throat
(and also,
            so subtly,
                        swipe them
                                    from their neighbours).

What
          can I say
                    about such
                              lyrical castration?
These folk
          who steal lines
                    and don't give a toss:
I suppose
          in a country
                    with this much peculation
they're happy
                    that
                              it's someone else's loss.
These stolen odes
                    stir the crowd
                              to a frenzy,
but history
                    will sort out
                              the chef
                                        from the waiters,
will mark down
                    these typists
                              under 'overhead expenses'
to support
          us two or three
                              truly
                                        talented writers.
You have to eat
                    your salt –
                              a hundredweight –
and smoke
          a hundred
                    horrid
                              cigarettes
just to dredge up
                    one
                              valuable word

from the deepest
                    human
                              depths.
So lower all the taxes
                    and wipe the nought
from the end
          of your statement
                              on inflation:
a ton of salt –
          one rouble and eight;
a hundred fags –
          one rouble ten.
So many
     questions
               on your
                    questionnaire:
'Have you stayed at home?'
                    'Have you travelled around?'
And what if,
          over the
               last
                    fifteen
                         years,
you've ridden
          ten Pegasuses
                    into the ground?
Or else,
     look at things
               from my side
                    for a second
and think
     about
          company size
               and property:
what if,
     at one and the same time,
               I find

I'm the people's leader,
                    and their employee?
Every word
          we speak
                    shows our
                              social class,
and we,
        the proletarians,
                          control the pen.
But
    one's soul
              gets worn out
                            over the years:
'He's done his useful work, it's the archive for this one!'
It gets harder
              to love
                      and harder
                                to express
myself:
        trying to do both,
                          my head spins.
Heart
      and soul
              both traded
                          at a loss,
the worst of all possible
                          amortisations.
When the sun
            heaves itself up
                            like a fattened hog
to illuminate
              the future
                        that's cripplefree
                                          and beggarless,
I'll be dead
            in a ditch,
                        I'll lie
                                and rot

along with dozens
                    of my former colleagues.
But when
          the time comes
                    to work out my probate,
I tell you this,
                and I tell the truth,
that out
        of all
              today's
                      reprobates
I'm
    the
         only
              one
                  with any worth.
We have to roar
                with a foghorn voice
in the philistine pea-souper,
                            or where the winds blow rough:
the poet
         is always
                  in debt
                          to the universe
and pays his percentage
                        in sweat and in grief.
I'm in debt
            to where I was born, to Baghdati;
I'm in debt
            to Broadway,
                        the street paved with light;
I'm in debt
            to the cherries
                           of Japan;
                                    to the Red Army;
to any subject
               about which
                           there's still to write.

But why
          do I
                    dress up as an artist anyway?
Just to
          spit out rhymes
                              and make
                                        crazy rhythms?
The word
          of a poet
                    is your immortality,
comrade taxman,
                    it's your resurrection.
Read
          this poem
                    in a hundred years,
and summon up
                    remembrance
                              of things past:
this day
          will live again,
                              this tax inspector,
this smell of ink,
                    this sun…
                              These things will last.
I know you're a convinced citizen of today,
but
          go get a ticket
                    to immortality –
                              run! –
and when
          you calculate
                    my poems' efficiency,
compound
          the interest
                    over a millennium.
And a poet's
          power

doesn't halt
            at this extent,
that the future'll
            remember you
                    rather than forget.
No, a rhyme
        is also
            powerful
                in the present:
a caress,
        a slogan,
                a knout,
                    a bayonet.
Comrade inspector,
            I'll give you my best:
cross out
        all the noughts
                    in your accounts.
And I demand
        as of right
                to be assessed
among
        the poorest
                workers and peasants.
And
    if
        you think
                that my explanation
puts someone else's
                words in your mouth,
then by all means...
                here's my fountain pen...
you're welcome...
                write something yourself...

·1926·

To Comrade Nette*

To the man and the ship

This was no nonsense from the beyond –
                  of course it made me shudder.
There turned into the port,
              melt-hot as summer its begetter,
comrade *Teodor*
Nette.
It's him.
        It's him I recognise.
The thick round glasses of the lifebelts.
'Hey there, Nette!
          I'm so happy you're alive
with the smoky life of funnels,
              gaffs and cables.
Come over here!
         Or is your draft too great?
From Batumi,
      perhaps,
          with your whistling boilers…
    Do remember,

---

* Teodor Ivanovich Nette (1896–1926), Revolutionary soldier and political officer. Mayakovsky introduced this poem in one of his readings thus: 'Nette, our diplomatic courier, was killed in Latvia in the line of duty, shot during an ambush by counterrevolutionaries. I knew Comrade Nette well. He was a stocky Latvian, with a pleasant smile and large horn-rimmed spectacles. I met him many times. I once had to travel abroad with him in the same train carriage. The poem also contains the name of Roman Jakobson, a mutual friend of us both. In the street in Rostov I heard the newsboys shouting: "Attack on our diplomatic couriers Nette and Makhmastal." I stopped dead. This was my first meeting with Nette after his death. Soon after this the initial pain subsided. One day I find myself in Odessa. I get a steamship to Yalta. When our steamer left Odessa, we meet another one coming in, with two words on it, in golden letters and illuminated by the sun: "Teodor Nette". This was my second meeting with Nette, but now not with the man, but with the steamer.' Reported in Pavel Lavut, *Mayakovskii edet po Soyuzu: Vospominaniya* (Mayakovsky Travels Around the Union) (1963).

back when you were human,
                              Nette
how we drank tea
                    in the diplomatic car?
You drank slowly.
                    The others snored on.
You kept cocking an eye
                              at the wax seals
as you chattered away
                    about Romka Jakobson
and tried to learn a poem,
                              sweating bullets.
Towards morning
                    you drifted off,
                              finger on the trigger…
Interrupt us
          if you dare!
Did you ever think
                    that
                              within a year
I'd meet you again
                    as a steamer?
A large moon
          mooning
                    behind your stern.
Great!
      It set,
          cutting space in half.
Because of your fight in the corridor
you will trail heroism behind you,
                              bright and bloody,
                                        forever.
Most people
          can believe
                    communism out of a book.
'Amazing
          what you can pick up just from reading!'
But an action

like this
             vivifies all this 'cock
and bull',
             and shows us communism,
                              real and bleeding.
We live,
          gripped by the iron oath
                         we swore.
We would go to the cross
                   or be shot
                            for our piety.
We want a world
               with no Russia
                       or Latvia:
to live in a single human society.
In our veins there is blood,
                         not water diluted.
We walk past the pistols and their yapping,
in order that
             when we die
                       we may be embodied
in ships,
         in poems,
                  in whatever lives long.

———

I want to live and live,
                   flashing through the years.
But in the end I want –
                 no other wish could be better –
to meet with death,
                as I count my final hours,
in the same way as comrade Nette.

· 15 July 1926 ·

A Letter from the Writer
Vladimir Vladimirovich Mayakovsky to the Writer
Aleksei Maksimovich Gorky

Aleksei Maksimovich,

              you'll remember

                         that between us

                                    there was

a quarrel,

       a tussle,

              an argument,

                     a fuss.

After which

          I went off

                 in my ripped trousers

and you

         soothed your scratches

                  in international spas.

Now everything
is very different.
The hair at my temples is grey

                and my eye

is bright.

         I'm not coming to see

                  the moralist or the saviour,

but – no irony –
the writer,

        speaking as a brother writer.

I'm very sad indeed, comrade Gorky,
not to see you

          in your hard hat

                here where we build our days.

Do you think

        that you

             are visible to gawk at

from the tops
            of the hills
                        in Capri?
You and Lunacharsky*
                        are generally praised,
good old chaps,
                        shamelessly writing;
commendable page
                        after commendable page
appears all day long.
What's so great about that?
What's there to be proud of?
They sell
            Cement
                        from every shop.
What value
            would you assign
                                    to such a testament?
No cement anywhere
                        and yet Gladkóv †
wrote a thanksgiving service
                                    for cement.
You stop up your nostrils,
                        wrinkle your nose,
and walk
            a mile
                        through squelch and stink.
In the meantime,
                        they say you quite approve
of that
            new novel

---

*   Anatoly Vasilievich Lunacharsky (1875–1933), art critic, journalist, and
Soviet Commissar for Education (1917–29).
†   Fiodov Gladkóv (1883–1958), author of the classic Soviet 'production
novel' *Cement* (1925).

about life as a monk.[*]
Few people
          know
                    how to write clean and simple,
          how to describe
                    a flowering radish
                                   or a sunset.
And so,
          when the soul
                    freezes to one's ribs,
          how can you try
                    to warm it!
The life of poetry
flows too quietly.
Where's the fire?
                    In their cold
                              and swoony-feeble verse
there's not even anything
                              pungently
                                        rotten
Anyone
          can pour
                    their feelings into chopped-up prose
and see it in the latest magazines.
And
          professor
                    Shengeli[†]
                              teaches
          the blacksmiths
                    anapaests.
          It's impossible

---

[*] Reference to *Relics* (1925), by Iosif Fiodorovich Kalinnikov (1890–1934). This was the first volume of what was eventually a four-volume novel, described as a 'semi-pornographic novel of monastic life', and published between 1925 and 1930.
[†] Georgi Arkadievich Shengeli (1894–1956), poet and critic. As author of the guidebook *How to Write Essays, Poems and Stories* (1926), he was fiercely criticised in Mayakovsky's essay 'How to Make a Poem'.

to understand,
                    you scratch
your head:
                    are you in a school
                                or a pub?
Aleksei Maksimovich, tell me:
have you ever seen the like over in Italy?
Domestic kitsch, conformity,
prix fixe activities and such-like jism
are described by many as 'healthy
realism'.
And we are
                    realists,
                                but not sheep safe at pasture,
not grazing
                    the grass
                                that grows at our feet:
we live in a new,
                    progressive future,
the world
                    of communism
                                and electricity.
It is only we
                    who do not praise
                                hackwork,
but who drag
                    the history
                                of literature
                                            on,
loading the years
                    on our backs:
it is only we
                    and some of our friends.
We are
                    no comfort
                                for the eyes
                                            or ears
                                                    of anyone.

We are LEF:
                  without twitching or nerves
we firmly and decisively
                        follow the ground-plan
to build tomorrow's world.
Our friends
            are the poets
                        of the working class.
Their knowledge may not yet
                        be enormous,
but their instinct
                  has built
                        a chorus of many voices
from the words
            of future years.
Gorky the emigrant's a thought we find bitter.
Justify your role with us, speak up in thunder!
I know
        that the powers that be
                              and the party
                                    highly rate you,
they'd give you anything,
                  from love
                        to a studio.
In the schoolroom
                  before you
                        would sit
                              the prose writers:
'Study!
        Study!'
Do you want to live like Chaliapin lives,*
ruined by applause, stifled?
If such an artist,
                  simply in search of roubles,
were now to come back,

* Fiodor Chaliapin (1873–1938), famous Russian operatic bass.

I'd be the first
           to shout:
                 'Go away,
                       People's Artist of the Republ-
ic!'
Aleksei Maximitch, through your windows can
you still see a soaring falcon?
Or have you decided to make
friends with the creeping snake?
The current rumour is, they say,
that you don't come 'cos you've got T B.
But you're in Europe,
                 where grub
                       and cash
                             and comfort
rots the core of every citizen!
Isn't our air cleaner,
                 twice rarefied
by the storm of two revolutions!
To leave
      the drama
           and rebellions
                       of the Republic
and tan
      your bald patch
                       under the southern sky:
shouldn't you rather
                 give your heart to your fractured epoch?
isn't it better
           to live
                 like Dzerzhinsky?*
Here,
      we're in work
                 up to our browlines,

* Felix Edmundovich Dzerzhinsky (1877–1926), revolutionary and head of
the Soviet secret police. A dubious role model.

our sleeves
              rolled up
                        to the elbow,
crimson flags in the skies,
                              and motorised steel falcons
keep a watch for the imperial eagle.
With deeds
              and blood
                        and lines
                                  of a kind
never before available to us,
I praise the flag,
                    raised like a beacon up high;
the flag of October,
                      insulted and glorified,
the red flag pierced with bullets!

·1926·

Jew

To my comrades in the OZET *

It used to be,
              you started
                            talking about Jews,
and your interlocutor
                      had some pretty odd views:
'Jews! In the bourse!
Lined up in rows!
Jews means currency,
Jews means scratch.
Fiercely greedy
And fiercely rich.
And now théy are
being given Crimea!
And everyone's aware
what a jewel Crimea is:
all that there is there
is palaces and roses.'
That's how
          the enemies' voices lie,
but you,
        worker,
              in all honesty,
should look
          directly
                  into the eye

---

* OZET: The Jewish Workers' Cooperative Land Designation Society.
After the Revolution, the Soviet Jewish community sought the designation
of an area in which Jews could live without fear of persecution. Mayakovsky's
poem, a summary of the various persecutions Jews faced under the tsars and
during the Russian Civil War, and a description of the successes they were
having in the Crimea, was written for a benefit evening on 17 November
1926. The Jewish Autonomous Oblast was set up round Birobidzhan, in the
extreme far east of Russia, in 1934.

of Jewish poverty.
Over the Pale of Settlement,

                    until this day,
one could still

          hear the echoes

                    of groans and cries.
The tsar's

          whips

                    and bullets

                              given free rein:
the 'yids'

          punished

                    for being rebellious.
As if you could set down

                    the blood that leaked
into the calculations

                    of statistical

                              tables.
The down

          from the slashed

                    feather-beds

                              of Bialystock,*
and the gouged-out eyes

                    where it sticks

                              and settles.
Scarcely holding back tears,

                    the sun looked on,
one eye

          with a vast

                    jaundiced pupil,
and saw

          how world war

                    gave way

---

*   Between 1–3 June 1906 a pogrom, provoked by the Russian authorities, led to the deaths of around eighty Jews in Bialystock, and injuries to eighty more.

           to a pogrom:
Germans
    and Russians
        and mobs of Poles.
And then came the 'democrats'
        and the Civil War:
they thundered
      by night
        and by day.
The groaning cannons
        overseen by Petliura;
the whipcrack
    of Makhno's*
        army.
Then,
   their homes
      still wet from their tears,
the Jews
   crept out
      from where they'd been hiding.
And the
    English-run
        department stores
sold them
    expensive
      rotten
        herring.
And again
   the stench
      of these local hells,
and uncleaned blood
      red as copper.

---

* Simon Vasilievich Petliura (1879–1926), a significant figure in the struggle for Ukrainian independence after the Russian Revolution, fomented a number of pogroms. Nestor Ivanovich Makhno (1888–1934), anarchist leader of the Revolutionary Insurrectionary Army of Ukraine, alleged instigator of several pogroms.

Then famine came
                    and started to call:
'Land, or death!
                    Land and labour!'
There was no sea,
                    not a bush,
                              not a village here,
the worst
        of all
                    Russia's bad spots:
when they came,
                    the wretched settlers
only planted
            tents made from
                            sail-cloth sheets.
Which locust was it, that in its zeal
devoured this desert?
Salt marsh gave way to weeds
which gave way again to salt.
Who measured
            the penance
                        paid by their labour?
There was heroism
                in every plume
                            of smoke
                                    to rise,
in every drop of water,
every chimney,
            every tile.
But here,
        now,
            a blue stream flows;
the drops of sweat
                that fell like hailstones
have given life to the soil,
and grapes
        hang in juicy bunches
                            from the vines.

People can look at work
                         with a calm mind:
look at the Jew
                 who has polished
                                   this ground.
The commune's words
                     grow into deeds
                                      and thrive:
look and tell me –
                    it's rare that you might –
which one
          of any two people
                             is the Slav,
and which one
               is the Semite.
We'll not let gossip
                      make us beasts
                                      by association.
We open our hearts
                    and modest wallets
                                         for this cause:
the coming life
                 with no races or nations,
the coming life
                 with no beggars or wars!

· 1926 ·

Beer and Socialism

A drunk throws up.
                A willow tree lists.
The mugs
        volcanoing:
                the ash is foamy.
On the mugs
        the inscription:
                'Crayfish
and beer from the Bebel* factory.'
A good joke!
           Witty!
                But it's also hurtful
(makes you feel rather liverish)
that Bebel has died,
                that the old man can't tell
how famous
        and well-remembered he is.
Anticipating
        drunken accidents
                in the future,
just so there's no doubt on that score,
children
        should know
                this king of liquid Bavaria,
this famous Marxist brewer.
In a year
        Bebel
           will have fallen out of his time:
they'll spread
        ridiculous
                biographical rubbish:
'For you

* Friedrich August Bebel (1840–1913), socialist politician, one of the founders of the German Social Democratic Workers' Party.

he might mean
Women and Socialism,
for us, he's beer and crayfish.'
As they gossip,
the women in the factory
already
know how
to describe
their menfolk:
'Yeah,
he's friends with Bebel,
if you know what I mean;
Bebel
matches him
drink for drink!'
In the filth,
as though it were a feather bed,
a man lies down,
his wits enfeebled,
and nobody says:
'He's pissed off his head',
but rather:
'He's completely bebeled!'
Marx
couldn't
have imagined better futures:
Absolut Engels;
Lassalle's House of Pancakes!
And you,
comrades,
what about you,
sirs?
Are you completely baked?
Comrade,
stamp this request
on your cranium,
so it stays

where it is
and doesn't disappear:
drop the custom
(it's a stupid custom!)
of naming things
after your masters.
Such attributions hang around day and night:
for the average brain it's like they're carved in granite.

·1927·

Letter to Tatiana Yakovleva*

In a kiss on the hands,
a kiss on the lips,
the trembling of a dear body,
the red
of my republics
should also burn brightly.
I do not like
Paris love:
put enough silk on any woman
and I stretch out,
doze off,
say 'down, boy'
to the eager puppy of passion.
You are
the only person
tall as me –
you stand
brow-to-brow

* Tatiana Alekseyevna Yakovleva (1906–1991), model and milliner, the daughter of White Russian émigrés, had an intense relationship with Mayakovsky in Paris.

next to me:
let me tell
this important evening's
story
in a straightforward
human
way.
At five o'clock all's somnolent;
the city-forest's fallen silent:
you scarcely hear a moan, or
just the whistled argument
of trains to Barcelona.
Lightning
stamps its foot
in the black sky,
the thunder curses –
a theatrical production:
this is no storm,
but jealousy,
like faith,
moving mountains.
Don't believe
the raw words
the other émigrés use,
don't be afraid
of their pusillanimity:
I'll put a rein on it,
I will tame the views
of these sprigs of the nobility.
Passion's measles
may leave scars,
but joy
is permanently
joy,
I will talk in verse,
for a long time,
very simply.

Jealousy,
              wives,
                        tears...
                                  enough!
My eyelids swell
                   like I'm some fantastic monster.
It's not for me,
                  I'm jealous on behalf
of Soviet Russia.
I've seen your shoulders,
                          the scars where consumption
has licked you,
                panting.
That's not our fault:
                       a hundred million
suffered
          equally
                   badly.
We are gentle with those who suffer now:
you can't force people to be better;
we need to have you
                     with us
                              in Moscow,
there aren't enough long-legged girls there.
On those legs
               you've been
                            through snow
                                          and typhus:
it's not right that here,
                          in Paris,
you should surrender them
                           to
                              the suppertime caresses
of the oil barons.
Don't think about it too much,
                                don't rumple
your eyes
           beneath

your straightened brow.
Come into my vast
　　　　　and clumsy arms
where they open
　　　　　as a crossroads.
You don't want to?
　　　　　Winter here,
　　　　　　　　if you must stay,
and we'll mark it down
　　　　　as one more
　　　　　　　　insult
　　　　　　　　　　on account.
But I will come back
　　　　　to take you one day,
with Paris or without.

·1928·

'*Productivity…*'

Productivity
　　　　　and a living wage
are recto and verso
　　　　　of the same page.

·1928·

Monte Carlo

The world
            is silent
                        from its head to its feet.
The sea
        lies still
                    in place.
People are asleep.
                        Horses are asleep.
Also asleep:
                the town of Nice.
Only here
            in the night's
                            black gauze
do headlights
                brightly sparkle –
on its way
            to Monte Carlo cruises
a high-end automobile.
Smoke
        over the sea
                        is like fluff;
there's a constant
                    noise
                            like arguing
in the bay:
            it's the yachts that drive
with their cargo
                of Americans.
The gambling palaces of Monaco's scion…
Sheep of the world, it's time to get shorn!
Years upon them,
                    weighing down –
eighty-seven
                if she's a day! –
Queens of Diamonds
                    blow their fortunes,

whatever system they play.
Showing off
            how much she's winning,
looking slyly
            to one side:
the Queen of Hearts observing
the fall
            of the Queen of Spades.
Fat as seals,
cheeks puffed and glowing,
living, real
aces and kings.
The ball jumps
                in the spinning roulette,
hands throw francs
                    into the pot:
orphelins, voisins du zéro…
Banknotes
            make the pockets bulge:
he can pick them out
                    by touch!
There's a capitalist for you.
There,
        and there,
                    a thief and a loafer,
one of the many
                hard-headed
                            idle,
throwing his cards in
                    with the others,
divvying up
            the world
                    they stole.
After the setting
                of the sun,
brains
        poisoned
                by sums,

the network
> of branches
>> hung
with the bankrupt ones.
The gambling itch
> scratched by morning,
they leave
> and crawl away.
When they see
> the horizon
>> dawning,
they crawl off
> and so do I.
The morning seeped
> through the stars;
we were shown up
> grubby
>> as the dawn rose,
like dirt
> on a typed
>> pink
>>> carbon:
Monte Carlo, grandiose
with its lousy montecharlatans.

·1929·

Lines on the Soviet Passport

I would
        tear through
                bureaucracy
                        like a wolf.
For credentials
        I have no respect.
I'd send paperwork
        straight to hell,
                along with
the horse it rode in on.
                But this document…
The polite functionary
                moves
along the frontier
        of cabins
                and compartments.
People
        proffer
                passports
                        and I give
my little purple booklet.
Some passports
                make him
                        show his teeth.
Others
        he almost disdains.
And with respect he takes e.g.
the double-dormant
                English lions.
With his eyes
        he eats
                the good ol' boy up,
and bends
        in a ceaseless obeisance,

and takes,
            as though
                        accepting a tip,
a passport that's an American's.
Looks at a Polish pass
                        like a goat at an advert.
His eyes
        bulge
                as he looks at the Pole's passport,
in dull
        elephantine
                        police-ishness,
where's this guy from,
                        and what
are these geographical fantasies?
Without turning
                    his cabbage-like bonce,
showing
        no feelings
                    in any way,
he unblinkingly takes
                        the passports
                                    of Danes
and all other kinds
                    of Scandi.
And suddenly,
            as if he's been burnt,
the fellow's mouth contorts.
The functionary
                takes hold of
                            my enormous,
                                        red-skinned
passport.
He holds it
            as though
                        it were a bomb

or a double-bladed razor
                          or a porcupine;
he holds it
          as though
                    it were a six-foot-long
rattlesnake
          with twenty fangs.
The porter
          winks
                    meaningfully:
he'll carry
          my luggage
                    free of charge.
The gendarme
          looks at the detective
                              questioningly;
the detective
          looks back
                    at the gendarme.
Oh,
     what joy
               it would give
                         the gendarme class
to flog
     and crucify me
                    on the spot
for having
          in my hand
                    such a hammer-nosed,
sickle-cheeked
               Soviet
                    passport.
I would
     tear through
               bureaucracy
                    like a wolf.

For credentials
                I have no respect.
I'd send paperwork
                    straight to hell,
                                    along with
the horse it rode in on.
                        But this document...
I draw it out
            from my wide trousers,
a
  priceless
            burden.
Read it and weep,
                you suckers:
I'm a citizen of the Soviet Union.

·1929·

I'm Happy!

Citizens!
        Great joy!
                Glad tidings!
Sympathetic people
                    should all smile along with me.
I need to share my joy,
                  that goes without saying,
and I will share it
                via the medium of poetry.
Today,
        like an elephant,
                  I breathe with ease;
when I walk
            my tread is light;
the night sped by
                like a wonderful dream,
with no need to cough
                or spit.
My pleasure levels
                are immensely increased.
These autumn days
                are a scented bath
and the roses
            (forgive the cliché)
                    bloom for me
and I,
        you'll have guessed,
                  give them a good sniff.
They're pretty special now,
                my rhymes
                    and thoughts:
they knocked
            the socks off
                my editor.

I'm now
          as hardy
                    and healthy
                              as a horse
or even –
          dare I say it? –
                              a tractor.
My budget
          and my stomach
                              are balanced,
strengthened
          and both in excellent shape.
I've made savings –
                    a serious number of percent –
and I'm healthier
                    and I've put on weight.
As if piece
          after piece
                    of the airiest cake
were laid
          on my tongue's
                    taste-cells:
that is the fairy-like
                    taste
                              I can taste
in my mouth's
          sweet-smelling
                              halls.
My head's
          always
                    clean on the outside,
now it's clean on the inside too,
                              and it shows.
I can write
          more pages
                    every day

than Tolstoy
>> ever used
>>>> to blow his nose.
Women surround me
>>>> in their polka-dot attire,
they want me
>>>> to tell them all about me,
I've become
>> a definite
>>>> wit and raconteur,
the life
>> and soul
>>>> of the Party.
I don't get sick
>>>> or stuck in bed.
I'm pinker
>>>> and my face
>>>>>> is fuller.
Citizens,
>> are you keen
>>>> to know my secret?
Shall I tell you?
>>>> Shall I?
Citizens,
>> you think
>>>> I'm wasting your time,
you're ready to hit me...
>>>> Just joking!
Don't worry,
>> I'll tell you my secret:
>>>>>> I –
just this morning –
>>>> gave up smoking.

·1929·

The Witching Hour...[*]

The witching hour by now you must be asleep
In the night like the silver river Oka the Milky Way
There's no cause for me to wake you up
Upset you with lightning telegrams I'm in no hurry
as they say the case is closed
the boat of love wrecked on the dull beat of life
Now you and I are even there's no cause
to go through our mutual pain insult and grief
Look at the calm spread over the world
The night's paid the sky its tribute of stars
at times like this time to stand up and unfold
to the years all history and the universe

·1930·

* This poem, perhaps a planned section of another long poem, was found among Mayakovsky's papers after his death. He quoted the middle four lines in his suicide note, changing the phrase 'Now you and I are even' to 'Now life and I are even'.

Acknowledgements

Versions of some of these translations have appeared in *Areté* and *The Wolf*.

Catriona Kelly and Tim Binyon were the first people to get me properly interested in Mayakovsky. Rosy Carrick, Boris Dralyuk, Edmund Griffiths, Jeremy Noel-Tod, James Rann and Artem Serebrennikov have all had useful or supportive things to say about these translations. Above all, thanks to Marian, for being a) supportive and b) patient.

Index of Titles and First Lines

Titles are in *italic*.